Mercy

WHAT EVERY CATHOLIC SHOULD KNOW

Salvation

Literature

God

Mercy

Being Catholic

Mercy

WHAT EVERY CATHOLIC SHOULD KNOW

Daniel Moloney

IGNATIUS PRESS
San Francisco

AUGUSTINE INSTITUTE
Greenwood Village, CO

Cover Design: Ben Dybas
Reprinted 2021.
©2020 Ignatius Press, San Francisco,
and the Augustine Institute, Greenwood Village, CO
All rights reserved.
ISBN 978-1-950939-15-2 (pbk)
ISBN 978-1-950939-14-5 (hbk)
ISBN 978-1-64229-122-3 (eBook)
Library of Congress Control Number 9781950939152

Printed in the United States of America ∞

Contents

1

His Mercy Endures Forever

Praise the LORD, for he is good;
    for his mercy endures forever; . . .
Who alone has done great wonders,
    for his mercy endures forever;
Who skillfully made the heavens,
    for his mercy endures forever.

—Psalm 136:1, 4–5

When this psalm was sung in the Temple in a chorus, the cantor would sing the first part of the verse, and the people would respond with the refrain "for his mercy endures forever." We can imagine ourselves singing in such a choir, getting into the rhythm, and being filled with the consoling thought that God's mercy endures forever. But the psalm takes a surprising turn:

Who struck down the firstborn of Egypt,
    for his mercy endures forever; . . .
But swept Pharaoh and his army into the Red Sea,
    for his mercy endures forever; . . .
Who struck down great kings,
    for his mercy endures forever;

Slew powerful kings,
>   for his mercy endures forever;
Sihon, king of the Amorites,
>   for his mercy endures forever;
Og, king of Bashan,
>   for his mercy endures forever. (Ps 136:10, 15, 17–20)

The death of all the firstborn of Egypt is an act of divine mercy? How does this make sense? How could the deaths of kings or the annihilation of an army be signs of God's mercy?

It is instructive to consider that God himself justifies his destruction of sinners in the name of his love and mercy. When Israel was commanded to place the pagan tribes under the ban, for example, God explains this command as revealing his mercy:

> When the LORD, your God, brings you into the land which you are about to enter to possess, and removes many nations before you—the Hittites, Girgashites, Amorites, Canaanites, Perizzites, Hivites, and Jebusites, seven nations more numerous and powerful than you—and when the LORD, your God, gives them over to you and you defeat them, you shall put them under the ban.... This is how you must deal with them: Tear down their altars, smash their sacred pillars, chop down their asherahs, and destroy their idols by fire. For you are a people holy to the LORD, your God; the LORD, your God, has chosen you from all the peoples on the face of the earth to be a people specially his own.... It was because the LORD loved you and because of his fidelity to the oath he had sworn to your ancestors, that the LORD brought you out with a strong hand and redeemed you from the house of slavery, from the hand of Pharaoh, king of Egypt. Know, then, that the LORD, your God, is God: the faithful God who keeps covenant mercy to the thousandth generation toward those who love him and keep his commandments,

but who repays with destruction those who hate him; he does
not delay with those who hate him, but makes them pay for it.
(Deut 7:1–2, 5–6, 8–10)

The practice known in the Near East as "the ban" (*herem*)
declared that no slaves or spoils be taken (Ex 34:11–17) and
often that all the men, women, and children of the conquered
peoples would be killed (Num 31:1–17; 1 Sam 15:1–10). In
this passage, God says that he commands this because of his
great mercy, love, and faithfulness.

This is not the first time God had associated mercy with
harsh treatment of others. In the passage from Deuteronomy
above, Moses reminds Israel of what God had already commanded back on Mount Sinai. Just after the incident with
the golden calf, Moses goes back up the mountain with God
and, mysteriously, asks to see God's glory. God agrees, and he
takes the occasion to say his divine name and describe himself
as merciful:

The LORD came down in a cloud and stood with him there
and proclaimed the name, "LORD." So the LORD passed before
him and proclaimed: The LORD, the LORD, a God gracious and
merciful, slow to anger and abounding in love and fidelity, continuing his love for a thousand generations, and forgiving wickedness, rebellion, and sin; yet not declaring the guilty guiltless,
but bringing punishment for their parents' wickedness on children and children's children to the third and fourth generation!
(Ex 34:5–7)

God emphasizes his mercy in one of the greatest moments of
intimacy in the Old Testament. He even prefaces his auto-
biographical description with his name, a mark of special
solemnity. But then immediately afterward, he proclaims a
ban against the pagans in the Promised Land:

> The LORD said: Here is the covenant I will make.... See, I am about to drive out before you the Amorites, Canaanites, Hittites, Perizzites, Hivites and Jebusites. Take care not to make a covenant with the inhabitants of the land that you are to enter; lest they become a snare among you. Tear down their altars; smash their sacred stones, and cut down their asherahs. You shall not bow down to any other god, for the LORD—"Jealous" his name—is a jealous God. Do not make a covenant with the inhabitants of the land; else, when they prostitute themselves with their gods and sacrifice to them, one of them may invite you and you may partake of the sacrifice. (Ex 34:10–15)

Unless one thinks God takes his own divine name in vain, the only interpretation of these passages is that God actually is merciful and that the ban expresses his mercy.

The God of Both Testaments

The word "mercy" (*hesed*) appears 250 times in the Old Testament, the fourth most used noun after "God/Lord," "soul," and "land." And yet, the ancient heresy of Marcionism declared that the God of the Old Testament was a God of justice and wrath, while the God of the New Testament was a God of mercy. In the popular mind today, the "God of the Old Testament" is placed in opposition to the "God of the New Testament," with the former being characterized by vengeance, destruction, rigor, and "strict justice," not mercy or love. Some people extend this division to the Trinity, believing that God the Father is the wrathful God of the Old Testament, while God the Son is the merciful God of the New Testament. The Church has condemned this idea. The Second Vatican Council's Dogmatic Constitution on Divine Revelation, *Dei Verbum* (November 18, 1965), insists upon the continuity of the Old Testament and the New: "The plan of salvation foretold by the sacred authors, recounted and explained by them, is found as the true word of God in the books of the Old Testament: these books, therefore, written under divine inspiration, remain permanently valuable.... God, the inspirer and author of both Testaments, wisely arranged that the New Testament be hidden in the Old and the Old be made manifest in the New" (14, 16).[1]

It is not as if the New Testament does not also promise some very "Old Testament" types of punishments. For example, Jesus threatens the cities that reject the preaching of the disciples with a punishment worse than that given to Sodom:

> Whatever town you enter and they do not receive you, go out into the streets and say, "The dust of your town that clings to our feet, even that we shake off against you." Yet know this: the kingdom of God is at hand. I tell you, it will be more tolerable for Sodom on that day than for that town. Woe to you, Chorazin! Woe to you, Bethsaida! ... It will be more tolerable for Tyre and Sidon at the judgment than for you. And as for you, Capernaum, "Will you be exalted to heaven? You will go down to the netherworld." Whoever listens to you listens to me. Whoever rejects you rejects me. And whoever rejects me rejects the one who sent me. (Lk 10:10–16)

He likewise references the people of Nineveh, who were threatened with their complete destruction, and says that the Ninevites will harshly judge those of the present day (Lk 11:32; Mt 12:41).

Some people assume that Jesus is a uniter rather than a divider. Yet in the Gospels he promises an even stricter separation from sinners than we see in the ban, namely, Hell. At the Last Judgment, Jesus will separate sinners from the saints and

---

1 Paragraph numbers, not page numbers, are used for all citations of official Church sources (i.e., Vatican II documents, encyclicals, and so forth).

will send the former to an eternal condemnation (Mt 25:46). Most of our teaching about Hell comes from Jesus' threats, and not from the Old Testament. Seven times Jesus threatens some people with being cast out to where there is "wailing and grinding of teeth" (Mt 8:12; 13:42, 50; 22:13; 24:51; 25:30; Lk 13:28). In addition, Saint Peter cursed a husband and wife for keeping back some of the money that they had pledged, and they died as a result (Acts 5:1–11). The Greek word *anathema*, which is used by Saint Paul to describe an excommunication (1 Cor 16:22; Gal 1:8–9), is the Greek translation of the Hebrew word for the ban (*herem*). Saint Paul tells Timothy regarding two heretical disciples, "I have handed [them] over to Satan." In so doing, Saint Paul believed he was acting out of mercy (1 Tim 1:20).

God's mercy is not what we expect it to be. Partially, that is because mercy is not what we expect it to be. The word "mercy" has taken on a host of connotations that do not make any sense, if we think about them. And those connotations in turn inform our sense of piety. If we think we understand what mercy is, then we think we know what the Church means when she says that God is merciful. Jesus tells us that our mercy should be measured by God's mercy (Lk 6:36), which means that our misunderstandings about God's mercy will also affect whether we live out our Catholic faith as Jesus commands.

Both defenders and critics of mercy often have mistaken ideas about it.

Mistakes by Defenders of Mercy	Mistakes by Critics of Mercy
Mercy is primarily a religious concept.	Mercy is irrelevant to politics.
Mercy is basically the same as being lenient.	Mercy is basically the same as being lax.

Mistakes by Defenders of Mercy	Mistakes by Critics of Mercy
The intolerant are not merciful.	Mercy toward the powerful is the opium of the masses.
Liberals are merciful; conservatives are not.	Mercy is aspirational but unrealistic.
Mercy requires us to open the borders.	Mercy is a force for chaos.
Mercy is identical to love.	Mercy is arbitrary.
The greatest thing about God is his mercy.	Mercy is optional.
Mercy is the opposite of justice.	To show mercy in the pursuit of justice is to compromise justice.
Mercy is about having good intentions and a good heart.	Too much mercy for bad priests caused the priest abuse crisis.
Mercy requires nonviolence.	Showing mercy puts us all in danger.

Over the course of the pages to come, we will have a chance to study these and other misconceptions about mercy.

The Law of Mercy

In the Gospel of Luke, Jesus teaches us to

> be merciful, just as [also] your Father is merciful. Stop judging and you will not be judged. Stop condemning and you will not be condemned. Forgive and you will be forgiven. Give and gifts will be given to you; a good measure, packed together, shaken down, and overflowing, will be poured into your lap. For the measure with which you measure will in return be measured out to you. (6:36–38)

The spiritual writer Father Jacques Philippe describes this teaching of Jesus as akin to one of the laws of physics. Just as Isaac Newton said that every physical action has an equal and opposite reaction, so here, in the Sermon on the Plain, Jesus is saying that our mercy toward our neighbor brings with it the proportional mercy of God, measure for measure. How we treat others determines how God will treat us.[2] Of course, this is not an impersonal or deterministic law but one laid down by a Person (a Trinity of Persons) with free will. Like the laws of physics, however, this "law" of mercy is unchanging—because the Person who promulgates this law is eternal and thus unchanging.

We must be merciful according to the standard of God's mercy toward us if we are to receive mercy from God. Jesus' account of the Last Judgment tells us what happens if we are not merciful: we will be condemned to eternal punishment. Yet in the Beatitudes, Jesus tells us that if we do show mercy, we will be shown mercy and will be blessed (Mt 5:7). There is, then, a kind of justice to God's mercy.

Jesus' exhortation to "be merciful, just as [also] your Father is merciful," suggests that the guide for our behavior must be God the Father's own divine mercy, and not mere human customs or emotions regarding mercy. We may have a great many preconceived notions about what it means to be merciful to one another, but Jesus' injunction means that we should reform our human conceptions in the light of what we can learn about divine mercy. In pursuit of that right understanding of mercy, this book will involve a constant back-and-forth between the human and divine, the natural and supernatural, politics and Scripture, state and church, with the goal of understanding what Jesus has called us to do.

---

2 Jacques Philippe, *The Eight Doors of the Kingdom: Meditations on the Beatitudes* (Cleveland, OH: Scepter Publishing, 2018), 142–43.

2

Mercy and the Nature of God

God is merciful, all Christians agree. But what does that mean? Theology allows us to say things about God that we cannot say about creatures. For example, we can say not only that God loves (which we can say about creatures) but also that God is the *source* of all love, and, what is more, we can say with Saint John (1 Jn 4:8) that he is love *itself*. We can say not merely that God is good but that God is the *source* of all that is good and that he is goodness *itself*. We can say that God is just, and also that he is the *source* of all justice, and that he is justice *itself*. The last claim in each example—that God is love itself, goodness itself, and justice itself—tells us something about the nature or essence of God, about what the three Persons of the Trinity have in common. If God is essentially love, then God the Father is love, God the Son is love, and God the Holy Spirit is love.

This makes God different from every creature, everything that is not God. You or I may be loving on some days and not on others. To love others is something we have to learn; it is an achievement. It is possible for us to look on some people or things with attitudes of hatred or indifference. We exist and remain who we are whether or not we are loving at a given moment. That is not the way it is with God. When we say that God is love, it implies that for him, loving is not something that he starts or stops doing; for him, to be is to love—love is what he is. Likewise, goodness is what God is, such that for God, to be is to be good. There cannot be any instant in which he is not totally and perfectly good. And the same with justice: justice is what God is. For God, to be is to be just.

Love, justice, and goodness may be called pure perfections. A pure perfection is (a) something that in creatures is perfecting in every case, and (b) something that can be said of an eternal and perfect God without introducing any sort of limitation or imperfection, or, as Saint Anselm put it, "whatever in every respect it is better to be than not to be." King Midas learned that turning some things into gold made them better but that turning his daughter into gold made her worse; hence, being gold is not a pure perfection. But it is always better to be good than not to be good, so goodness is a pure perfection.

Only pure perfections can be attributed to God essentially. In his *Monologion*, a celebrated discussion of God's nature, Saint Anselm gave us a long list of pure perfections: God is "Supreme Being (*summa essentia*), Supreme Life (*summa vita*), Supreme Reason, Supreme Refuge, Supreme Justice, Supreme Wisdom, Supreme Truth, Supreme Goodness, Supreme Greatness, Supreme Beauty, Supreme Immortality, Supreme Incorruptibility, Supreme Immutability, Supreme Beatitude, Supreme Eternity, Supreme Power, Supreme Oneness."[1]

Mercy was not on his list, because mercy is not a pure perfection.

Yes, God is merciful, but not *essentially*. In the same way, God is the Creator, but not essentially. God could have decided not to create anything, and he still would have been God, so being a creator cannot be essential to God. Mercy necessarily involves some sort of response to evil or imperfection. If you

---

1   Anselm, *Monologion* 16, trans. Jasper Hopkins and Herbert Richardson, in *Complete Philosophical and Theological Treatises of Anselm of Canterbury* (Minneapolis: Arthur J. Banning Press, 2020), 28, https://jasper-hopkins.info/monologion.pdf.

have to ask someone for mercy, it is because you are having a bad day. The Fatima Prayer speaks of those "most in need" of God's mercy, because mercy reflects some need. For mercy to exist, it implies a kind of relation toward creation; even more than that, it implies a fallen world in need of divine assistance. If mercy were essential to God, it would mean that God could not be God without being related to creation—to a *fallen* creation—but this is plainly not the case.

God is not eternally merciful, because things are not eternally awful. Before the first sin, everything God created was good. There was then no need for mercy. After Jesus comes again at the end of time to establish God's Kingdom definitively, everything will be right again and there will no longer be a need for mercy. The prophet Isaiah promises that when the Kingdom is established fully, God will "wipe away the tears from all faces" (25:8), and Saint John declares the same: there will be an end to the need for mercy (see Rev 21:4).

As the example of God as Creator suggests, there are many important attributes of God that are not essential to him. Mercy is one of them. It is important for us to know that God is merciful, even if it is not part of his nature. God has revealed his mercy to us for a reason. Pagan gods were known for their cruelty, not their mercy. The true God is different. Yet if God's mercy is not part of his nature, then there must be some aspect of God's nature that divine mercy makes manifest. The Catholic theological tradition tends to emphasize two: God's love and his powerful goodness.

Mercy, an Aspect of God's Love

Today, most would assume that mercy is closely related to charitable love, or that mercy is even another name for love. The phrase "God's merciful love" sounds right to us. It is a constant theme of Pope Francis, from his first Angelus address on March 17, 2013: God "is the loving Father who always pardons, who has that heart of mercy for us all." Pope Saint John Paul II, in his Encyclical Letter on the Mercy of God, *Dives in Misericordia* (November 30, 1980), identifies mercy and love: "The mystery of Christ, which reveals to us the great vocation of man … also obliges me to proclaim mercy as God's merciful love, revealed in that same mystery of Christ" (15). In a previous paragraph, he stated, "It is precisely because sin exists in the world, which 'God so loved … that he gave his only Son' (Jn. 3:16), that God, who 'is love' (1 Jn. 4:8), cannot reveal Himself otherwise than as mercy" (13).

The logic behind what the popes are saying is straightforward:

1. Jesus' Incarnation reveals the Father's love: "God so loved the world that he gave his only Son" (Jn 3:16).
2. Jesus became incarnate in order to suffer and die for us, and so save us.
3. Jesus' saving us is the greatest act of mercy.
4. Therefore, Jesus' act of mercy reveals God's love for us and that God's love is great.

That does not mean that mercy and love are the same thing. Mercy is only one aspect of God's love. God's love is broader than his mercy. Love is a pure perfection—mercy is not. The Persons of the Trinity all love each other, yet they do not show mercy to each other. God *loved* Adam and Eve before the Fall, but only after the Fall does he show them mercy, when the loss of divine friendship becomes a tragic lack that only God can rectify.

For us, however, mercy is the most powerful way God reveals his great love for us. God the Father sent God the Son to become flesh and die and rise and ascend to Heaven while still incarnate. In the Garden of Gethsemane, Jesus emphasizes that his death is the Father's will. This way of talking about mercy answers the question of God's motivation, of *why* he sent his Son on a mission of mercy: out of love.

When we say that God's mercy is an aspect of his love or that mercy reveals God's love, it calls our attention to a truth about God: "God is love" (1 Jn 4:8). Moreover, he loves us even when we are not all that lovable. God's love for us in our fallen state, when we are objectively unlovable, makes a great impression on us. It is one thing to love the lovable and the worthy and the good; it is another to love sinners and our enemies and the unlovable. Jesus' sacrifice on the Cross proves in a definitive way that God loves us in our fallen, sinful state, and that is surprising, marvelous, and very Good News. His mercy should fill us with thanksgiving, and we ought to love him back.

God's Mercy Is Not an Emotion or a Passion or a Feeling

Saint Isidore of Seville once made a famous observation about one of the Latin words for mercy, *misericors*. The word's etymology implies that the merciful person has a "sorrowing heart," so Saint Isidore argued that the word could not be used to describe God's mercy. As a spiritual being, God does not have a physical heart. Nor does he have a heart in the sense of the seat of emotions and passions, since God does not have anything like hormones or bodily passions to make him emotional.

Saint Isidore's point was that God's mercy is not to be thought of with human concepts such as being moved with sorrow. God is love, but God does not have an emotion or feeling of love. The same is true in general about God: he is weird and strange and much greater than we can conceive. Saint Augustine was so insistent that we not use anthropomorphic language about God that he spent decades writing his treatise *On the Trinity* in order to correct the theological language of his day: "It is difficult to contemplate and fully know the substance of God; who fashions things changeable, yet without any change in Himself, and creates things temporal, yet without any temporal movement in Himself. And it is necessary, therefore, to purge our minds [of false concepts of God], in order to be able to see ineffably that which is ineffable."[2]

Mercy, an Aspect of God's Goodness

The emphasis on mercy as an aspect of God's love is typical of our era in theology. There is another traditional understanding of mercy, however, that instead foregrounds mercy as an aspect of God's *powerful goodness*. Saint Thomas Aquinas defined mercy as God's goodness in removing defects and suffering in his creatures (*Summa Theologiae* I, q. 21, a. 3). Aquinas' argument also has a strong logic behind it:

1. Mercy includes the idea of responding to some suffering or defect in another.
2. The merciful person wants to remove the suffering or defect in the other.
3. To remove defects is to make something *better*.
4. To make something better is to make it *more good*.
5. Therefore, mercy is related to goodness.

---

2   Augustine, *On the Trinity* 1.1.3, trans. Arthur West Haddan, in *Nicene and Post-Nicene Fathers*, 1st series, vol. 3, ed. Philip Schaff (Buffalo, NY: Christian Literature Publishing, 1887), revised and edited for New Advent by Kevin Knight, 2020, https://www.newadvent.org/fathers/130101.htm.

Built into the very language of mercy is an idea of responding to some suffering or misery, which Aquinas defines generally as a *deficiency* of some sort. We can see what he means by noticing that the traditional list of the works of mercy mentions several types of deficiencies: nakedness is a deficiency of clothes, hunger comes from a lack of food, ignorance from a lack of instruction, and so on. Having a merciful heart makes one want to remove the deficiency in the other.

But "remove a deficiency" is a double negative; and just as in math, to subtract a negative is to add. To get rid of the badness of the deficiency, in other words, you have to add more goodness. To make something better, you have to make it more good. Not necessarily in the sense of moral goodness but in the sense that someone who has totally recovered from an illness might say, "I'm all better." Goodness here refers to being whole; the Latin word *perfectio* that Aquinas uses also has the connotation of being whole, of being completely what you should be, without missing anything. Whatever was wrong has been righted.

Aquinas concludes that mercy is just the name for a specific aspect of God's goodness, the part of God's goodness that remedies deficiencies, that rights wrongs. Divine mercy is enacted whenever God adds goodness to someone who is missing it in some way or—what amounts to the same thing—takes away a badness. Mercy is restorative.

Mercy Responds to Privations

Aquinas uses the word *defectus* (which we translate as "deficiency") to describe what mercy needs to remedy. A more precise term might be "privation." A privation is a lack of something that ought to be there. Blindness is a classic example of a privation, since to be blind is to not be able to see when you should be able to see. We would not say that a rock is blind, even though a rock cannot see, because rocks are not supposed to see.

Aquinas teaches that mercy is a response to a privation of whatever sort. It would not be mercy to give a man something he did not need, say, a blade of grass. We could regard it as a gift, and from a certain perspective we could regard it as a deficiency that the man did not have the blade of grass already. But because it would not be something that he lacked and ought to have had, it would not be a wrong that needed to be righted, a privation in the sense that we are using the word. So, giving it to him would not be an act of mercy. It would, however, be mercy to give him a meal when he is hungry, to give him knowledge when he is ignorant, and to help him go to Confession if he is in a state of sin. Any privation can be a wrong to be righted by mercy.

Mercy Reveals God's Omnipotence and Perfection

Thinking of mercy as the ability to make something better means that to be merciful you must also be powerful. It is not enough to want to do something to remove the privation; you have to be able to make a difference. You cannot be suffering from the same problem you are trying to remedy. You cannot help the poor if you do not have any money to give; you cannot bury the dead unless you are alive. The ability to provide the goodness that the other person needs implies that, in the relevant sense, you are strong enough to help.

Earlier we looked at how God's mercy reveals his love. This line of reasoning should lead us to realize that God's merciful goodness, which can make all things better and remedy all defects and privations, reveals his omnipotence. Since God is able to raise everything from imperfection to its perfection, he cannot be subject to any of the failings that he is able to fix. God's mercy thus reveals that he must be all-powerful and perfect in every way. This philosophical conclusion helps explain why, in Scripture, God's mercy is so often associated with God's strength, why his "great wonders" (Ps 136:4) and "mighty hand" (Ps 136:12) show that his mercy will endure forever (Ps 136:1–26).

Understanding God's Mercy Helps Us to Understand Human Mercy

Let us apply what we have learned about mercy to one of the classical spiritual works of mercy: instructing the ignorant. A catechism teacher facing a class of unruly seventh graders might be exasperated and cranky (as I can attest from personal experience). If mercy were an emotion, then it would seem that in the absence of the correct emotion the catechist could not perform a work of mercy. But that does not seem right. The catechist may not be overflowing with loving feelings and yet could still be doing good, making the relatively ignorant students less ignorant. If mercy only had to do with feelings, we would not want to count this as a work of mercy. But if mercy also has to do with making things better, then it clearly would count. In fact, it is not unthinkable that a really excellent teacher who makes the students much less ignorant, and who thus accomplishes great works of mercy, might also have an extremely difficult personality. Such a teacher's long-standing commitment to performing these works of mercy would reveal that, in his own curmudgeonly way, he was acting from love.

God's Merciful Good Actions Reveal His Merciful Love

Love and goodness are pure perfections, and so they can be said of God essentially: God is love itself and goodness itself.

Although this does not necessarily imply that our human concepts of love and goodness can be reduced to each other, it certainly means that love and goodness are not incompatible. It is not as if, say, advocates of Saint Thomas Aquinas' pro-goodness view of mercy have to condemn Pope Saint John Paul II's pro-love view, and vice versa. Both views are reasonable and true. There is a wideness in God's mercy, as the hymn tells us.

As a priest in pastoral ministry, I help myself to both traditions. When people with scruples think that God will not forgive them for their sins, I emphasize his merciful love. When people experiencing desolation think God will not help them make progress in their spiritual life, I emphasize his merciful goodness and point out that he is more powerful than their defects and failings. I encourage penitents to focus on God's love as a way of emphasizing his benevolent intentions for us and his solidarity with us as his sons and daughters. I encourage them to focus on his goodness to emphasize that his actions are always in the service of making things better. Even his punishments or his permitting suffering or his sending us the cross are for the good. I think that the best way for us to balance these two traditions is to start by teaching about God's goodness. Then we can highlight what God's actions teach us about God himself: that he loves us. Divine mercy happens when God acts to make something better, which shows his love for those in need.

3

Mercy—a Political Virtue

In our culture, mercy has almost exclusively religious connotations. People associate mercy with religious orders, popes, and hospitals. There is a complicated history behind this trend, but, for whatever reason, we have forgotten that mercy's home is in politics, as an attribute of kings and emperors. In both the Old and New Testaments, God's mercy is seen as an attribute of God's kingship, his governance of the whole universe. The Jews believed that, among the many other ways to think about God, he was the perfect king and that the perfect king shows mercy. This was one of the features that distinguished God from the false gods worshipped by the pagan nations: while they were cruel and arbitrary, God was always constant and "his mercy endures forever" (Ps 136:1–26). To understand mercy, we should understand what it was about this ancient political concept that made it helpful in understanding God.

In the year 27 B.C., the Roman Senate honored Caesar Augustus with a shield representing four virtues, one of which was *clementia*, or mercy. They did this presumably to remind the new emperor of the policy of his adoptive father, Julius Caesar, who was famous for granting clemency to those who opposed his seizure of power rather than executing them. The Roman senator Seneca the Younger, a philosopher and tutor to the emperor Nero, wrote a treatise, *On Mercy (De*

Clementia), in which he praised mercy as a virtue fit for kings, as it makes them more honored and their regime more stable than would be the case otherwise. (Nero, it should be noted, was not the best of pupils.)

As classically understood, mercy was the virtue for someone who had some sort of power relation to another, either power over another or the power to help another. It was closely related to the virtue of justice, which governed how things ought to be, especially between persons. As we have seen, mercy also had the connotation that there was something wrong about the person in need of mercy, that either forgiveness was needed for some misdeed or assistance was required for some plight.

A king shows mercy to his subjects when he mitigates a sentence that has been passed, when he makes an exception to a policy that adversely affects a particular person, when he replaces the strict laws of his predecessor with ones better adjusted to the habits of his subjects, when he gives liberally to the poor, or when he restores someone to the position in society that he had lost. A king who shows mercy is usually popular with his people; to say a ruler is merciless implies that he is cruel and unpopular. Later in history, as the legal courts obtained a certain functional independence from the court of the king, mercy became associated with the law as well so that one could throw oneself "on the mercy of the court."

God's Mercy Is Also Political

Shakespeare touches on all these traditional uses of mercy in a famous speech from *The Merchant of Venice*:

> The quality of mercy is not strain'd,
> It droppeth as the gentle rain from heaven

Upon the place beneath: it is twice blest;
It blesseth him that gives and him that takes:
'Tis mightiest in the mightiest, it becomes
The throned monarch better than his crown;
His sceptre shows the force of temporal power,
The attribute to awe and majesty,
Wherein doth sit the dread and fear of kings;
But mercy is above this sceptred sway;
It is enthroned in the hearts of kings,
It is an attribute to God himself;
And earthly power doth then show likest God's
When mercy seasons justice.[1]

Shakespeare here associates mercy with "the mightiest," "the throned monarch," who is most like God himself when he exercises mercy. Mercy is presented as the exercise of power in a gentle way for the good of those in one's power, a kindness to the recipient, and a virtue in the one who is merciful. The continuity between divine and human mercy is made explicit here: powerful people especially ought to be merciful as God is merciful. This point is an important one because we are liable to misunderstand mercy when we forget that it is primarily a political virtue.

If mercy is a political concept, it follows that mercy must contribute to and promote a just society, on earth and in Heaven. It cannot be the case that mercy is unjust, or that justice is merciless—not if they are both to be good and desirable, let alone if both are attributes of God. If it is coherent to talk about both divine justice and divine mercy, it cannot be the case that mercy leads to a less just society or an imperfect Heaven. If an idea about mercy does not make sense in

---

1   William Shakespeare, *The Merchant of Venice*, ed. Joseph Pearce, Ignatius Critical Editions (San Francisco: Ignatius Press, 2009), 4.1.184–97. (Numerals refer to act, scene, and lines.)

political and social life, then it will not make sense in theology or religious life either. If we take mercy seriously, we may have to think differently about God and about our politics, about the exercise of divine and human justice.

Christian Realism's Rejection of Mercy in Politics

The twentieth-century Protestant theologian Reinhold Niebuhr objected to the idea that mercy should have a role in politics and persuaded many people of the merits of what he called "Christian realism." Niebuhr believed that mercy could be a private virtue; a private citizen was free to turn the other cheek or even to acquiesce in martyrdom. But public authorities in the exercise of their public offices could not be bound to follow the commands of Gospel love. We must be free to meet force with force; we "must try in every social situation to maximize the ethical forces and yet not sacrifice the possibility of achieving an ethical goal because we are afraid to use any but purely ethical means."[2]

Niebuhr thought that the tragic lot of the responsible Christian politician in this life was to act in the world of power politics with all its messiness and moral impurity, while looking to the morally pure life of the Christian pacifist for a reminder of how the individual should treat his neighbor. In a famous exchange with his brother, H. Richard Niebuhr, also a theologian, Reinhold Niebuhr wrote,

> The hope of attaining an ethical goal for society by purely ethical means, that is, without coercion, and without the assertion

---

2   Reinhold Niebuhr, "Must We Do Nothing?", a critique of an article by his brother, H. Richard Niebuhr, entitled "The Grace of Doing Nothing," in the March 23, 1932, issue of *The Christian Century*, from the website of the United Church of Christ, https://www.ucc.org/beliefs_theology_must-we-do-nothing.

of the interests of the underprivileged against the interests of the privileged, is an illusion....

I realize quite well that my brother's position both in its ethical perfectionism and in its apocalyptic note is closer to the gospel than mine. In confessing that, I am forced to admit that I am unable to construct an adequate social ethic out of a pure love ethic. I cannot abandon the pure love ideal because anything which falls short of it is less than the ideal. But I cannot use it fully if I want to assume a responsible attitude towards the problems of society.[3]

This view is striking in its willingness to compromise the putative demands of God in response to the realities of the sinful world. A public official cannot allow himself to show mercy, because that involves accepting injustice, and his job is to promote justice. Mercy can temper justice, but only because mercy is opposed to justice, which always involves parties struggling to assert their interests.

Niebuhr's Christian realism holds that mercy and love are aspirational ideals but not political ones. They are characteristic of how things will be at the Second Coming but cannot characterize real life. The Christian realist regards the pursuit of sanctity as often incompatible with the demands of pursuing justice in a sinful world. The view that Christian mercy has a significant role to play in politics appears to the Christian realist to be utopian and irresponsible.

Yet as we have seen, the Gospels assert what we called a "law of mercy," that we ought to be merciful as God is merciful in order to receive mercy ourselves. So, which is it? Is mercy optional? Or is it a commandment and thus a duty? Is it essential to politics or disastrously irresponsible? These sorts of questions have been around for a while. But a satisfactory

---

3   Ibid.

account of mercy ought to be able to answer them. Some of the problems come from some easy-to-make mistakes about what mercy is and some corresponding mistakes about what justice is.

Mercy Is Not the Same as Leniency

Christian realists assume that mercy is identified with being lenient, with not applying a rule or a law in a particular case. This makes sense at first. If we ask for mercy from the court, we are not arguing that the court has committed some sort of error or injustice. We grant that the court is just; we merely want the sentence to be reduced or we want to be pardoned altogether. Nobody begging for mercy wants the law applied more strictly. So, mercy would seem to be the same as granting leniency.

This way of thinking can give mercy a bad name. In the 1980s, many state and federal judges decided that it was, in general, better to give criminals lighter sentences. But shorter sentences meant that the criminals quickly were back on the street, and many of them committed further crimes. The public thought that crime was out of control and demanded action. So, Congress and many state legislatures introduced sentencing guidelines that took away the judge's ability to impose a light sentence. In the name of "law and order," the legislators outlawed mercy, which they equated with leniency. This is why mercy worries realists: if mercy is a duty, then it would seem we must be lenient as a matter of duty, which is bad for society.

Christian realists assume that mercy is leniency and justice is strictness, and they reject mercy. But if mercy means "not to apply the law," then to apply the law would be merciless. If the law that is being applied is actually a good and just law, then not to apply it in the name of mercy would be to do something bad and unjust. This way of thinking defines mercy and justice as opposites. That is the essential problem. If both justice and mercy are virtues, then they cannot be contrary to each other. They must be defined in such a way that they can work together.

Unprincipled Mercy Seems Arbitrary

Christian realists think that one way to resolve this problem is to allow mercy to temper justice, to be lovingly lenient where possible, but not to treat mercy as a rule that one must follow. Both are virtues, and you should sometimes use one, sometimes the other. But how should we decide when to show mercy? Realists do not really have a systematic answer. This brings us to another problem, that of arbitrariness.

If mercy means not to apply the law, then either it invites arbitrariness or else it effectively amends the law in the direction of leniency. If a judge decides to show mercy to someone, he needs a good reason to do so, some morally relevant feature of the situation that justifies leniency. Otherwise, he is being arbitrary, which would be unjust. But if the judge has a good reason to show mercy in one case, then that would be a good reason to show mercy in all similar cases. For example, if he pardons one thief because he is from a broken family, then he should pardon every thief who comes from a broken family. But then, the judge has changed the law, and now it is permissible for people from broken families to steal. Presumably, if the legislature had wanted a more lenient law with all sorts of loopholes, it would have passed one. Defining mercy as "justified leniency" turns mercy into a one-way ratchet: once you show mercy in one case, leniency becomes the law. Otherwise, mercy is arbitrary and unjust.

The Case of Brother Tardy

Let us think of a simple example in a simple society. Brother Tardy is a Benedictine monk who routinely shows up late for Vespers. There are a variety of reasons for his bad habit: he gets too absorbed in the work that he is doing; he dawdles; he does not give punctuality much importance. But he is late almost every day. The abbot decides not to discipline Brother Tardy, thinking that he should show him mercy because "that is just the way he is." But as the abbot, he cannot have favorites. It would not be fair to discipline Brother Sleepy for being late when he let Brother Tardy off the hook. So, when the next person is late, he, too, is not punished. Well, you can imagine what would happen. Pretty soon, Vespers has to start late because too few people are there on time. (Why put down what you are doing when you have to wait for all the monks to gather anyway?) This in turn throws off the rest of the schedule, and so monks will start asking if they can say Vespers on their own in order to get on with their evenings. Eventually, all the monks will be praying Vespers on different schedules. The exercise of mercy (defined as leniency) leads to disorder.

The Pacifists Are Also Wrong about Mercy and Self-Defense

Another mistake of Christian realists is to assume that mercy requires pacifism, that using coercion and punishment and lethal force, even in the context of legitimate self-defense, is an unethical, sinful compromise of the commandment to love God and neighbor. The Christian pacifists who debate with Niebuhr (not only his brother, Richard, but more recently John Howard Yoder and Stanley Hauerwas) argue that since self-defense is an act of un-Christian violence, and since the

Gospel has force even in politics, it would also be un-Christian for political leaders to defend their countries. Christian realists like Niebuhr respond to this argument in two ways: either they disagree with the pacifists about whether mercy can be a political virtue or they bite the bullet and declare that sometimes the right thing to do is at the same time un-Christian.

The Church very much sides with the pacifists and against the realists: the political sphere is under the jurisdiction of the Gospel message because all men are called to imitate the mercy and love of God. Vatican II insisted on this point: everybody is called to holiness, public officials included. It is never right to do wrong, to do the un-Christian thing.

But does mercy really require abandoning self-defense, as the pacifists and realists both think? After all, God's mercy in the Old Testament led him to annihilate his opponents. And God justified his actions as necessary to defend Israel. The Church today also defends the right to self-defense and argues that killing others in self-defense is not a violation of the fifth commandment. *The Catechism of the Catholic Church* (*CCC*) states that "it is legitimate to insist on respect for one's own right to life. Someone who defends his life is not guilty of murder even if he is forced to deal his aggressor a lethal blow" (2264).[4] As Pope Saint John Paul II wrote in his Encyclical Letter on the Gospel of Life, *Evangelium Vitae* (March 25, 1995), echoing the Church's constant tradition, "The need to render the aggressor incapable of causing harm sometimes involves taking his life. In this case, the fatal outcome is attributable to the aggressor whose action brought it about" (55). By declaring self-defense to be a legitimate and therefore good action, the Church disagrees both with the pacifists, who deny the possibility, and with the Niebuhrian realists, who think that resisting aggressors is an evil, albeit a necessary one.

---

4   For all citations of the *Catechism*, numerals refer to paragraph numbers, not page numbers.

The realists think that mercy is a perfectly fine virtue for the individual saint, but not for the political leader in the real world. Being responsible for people other than oneself creates a different set of moral demands, they argue, and it would be wrong to ignore them. The Church agrees with their point about duty: "Legitimate defense can be not only a right but a grave duty for one who is responsible for the lives of others" (*CCC* 2265). There is a difference between my personal right to self-defense—which I can choose not to exercise—and the duty for those whose responsibility it is to defend the common good against unjust aggressors. Duties are not optional. And the Church calls the self-defense of society a particularly grave duty.

Legitimate Self-Defense Is Compatible with Mercy and Love

Legitimate "defense of the common good requires that an unjust aggressor be rendered unable to cause harm," says the *Catechism* (2265). This is the *incapacitating function of punishment*. Three traditional ways of incapacitating someone are imprisonment, exile, and death, but there are many others. One might regard taking away a drunk driver's license as a version of incapacitating punishment, or even sending a child to his room away from his brother.

This leads us to a key point: incapacitation is compatible with loving the person you incapacitate, as we can appreciate from the example of separating two unruly children. Even when using lethal force, it is not necessary to dehumanize or hate the other person. One can kill reluctantly in self-defense or out of a duty to protect others. If it is possible to defend society with coercive force and still love your enemy, then we can start to see how love and justice can be compatible.

Once we have protected the common good by rendering the aggressor unable to cause harm, we have a host of options. With society safe, we can turn to look at the aggressor to see if there is something we can do. We can help the alcoholic get treatment; we can help the warring brothers calm down and learn how to control their anger; we can even, sometimes, help the prisoner become a law-abiding citizen. In other words, incapacitating someone is compatible with helping him, with acts of mercy.

Catholic Realism

Legitimate self-defense introduces a measure of political realism into the exercise of mercy. It allows for the use of coercive force both domestically (in cases of punishment) and internationally (in cases of war). It also requires the exercise of political judgment about what sort of danger a person or group might possess. Are they a threat to society's order or to its very existence? Are they a major threat or a minor threat? Can they be persuaded to be an ally? What would that take? Is diplomacy enough? For that to happen, do we have to break their will to fight? Do we do that through appeals to their self-interest, or appeals to our strength, or both? Are they dangerous enough to be worth the bother of punishing? Is their side of the argument one we should take into consideration: Could we be wrong and they be right? Will our people back us in using coercive force in this case? Are we strong enough to win? Are we strong enough to be able to moderate our use of force and still win, or is their threat so great that we have to hit them with everything we have got? Can we be patient with them, or is their threat so great we need to act preemptively once they make threats?

A political conception of mercy is compatible with such considerations because mercy is not sentimental. Mercy is not the same as believing that the world is characterized by innocence. Everything was indeed created good by God, but after the Fall, it is not all good; rather, "sin lies in wait at the door" as God tells Cain (Gen 4:7). There is not a single aspect of the Christian message that is not a response to the world's evil, to its fallenness (see *CCC* 309). Mercy is not utopian. It is actually the opposite, for mercy is a virtue that comes into play when things go wrong. It is a virtue that is interested in righting wrongs, which means that to be merciful requires that one face up to the reality of evil and the difficulty of uprooting it.

To this point, we have talked about love and goodness and leniency and legitimate self-defense and realism. But if mercy is a response to things that are wrong, it logically depends on us having some idea of how things ought to be when they are right. In other words, mercy also requires us to think about justice.

4

Justice-Only Politics

Our culture is obsessed with justice. People today talk about all kinds of justice: criminal, economic, racial, environmental, legal, gender, international, distributive, restorative, commutative, procedural. What is more, as a society we get angry at injustice. Injustice is a wrong that must be righted! Injustice seems to be everywhere; to see it we need only be "woke," as people say today. Woke to white privilege, woke to the undermining of democracy, woke to police brutality, woke to microaggressions, woke to the patriarchy, woke to power of the 1 percent, and so on. People can become so alert to an aspect of justice that they see violations of it everywhere. They are angry at injustice and angry all the time.

Jesus promised that those who "hunger and thirst for justice" would be "blessed" and "happy" and "satisfied" (Mt 5:6, my translation). Being angry all the time seems like none of these. On the other hand, not to be angry also seems wrong, as if we do not care about justice. We can frame the problem by recalling a debate between two schools of ancient philosophy. Aristotle argued that under certain conditions there was a virtue in being angry. When the virtuous man determines that something is unjust, he should be angry at the injustice and want to correct it. To have the right amount of anger at the right things is to have righteous anger, a virtue; not to have it is the vice of indifference. If you see a child being verbally abused, or a dog being tortured, or you read about Christians being beheaded by ISIS, or Planned Parenthood selling off baby parts, should you be indifferent? "Oh well, another genocide. Please pass the bread." Aristotle saw anger as an emotion that helps move us to action, so not to be angry at injustice is to signal that you will not act to correct the injustice.

Activists of all stripes understand that "caring" is the beginning of change. If we are moved to anger by some injustice, it is easier to go through the inconvenience of fighting it. Vladimir Lenin's manifesto *What Is to Be Done?* encouraged the Bolsheviks to set up a network of newspapers that would highlight "atrocities against workers" in order to incite a Communist revolution in Russia. They did, and it worked. Politicized anger moves people to political action. That is why stories of injustice play such a large role in our politics, why negative political advertising is more effective than positive advertising.

Pervasive Injustice and the Danger of Scapegoating

Sometimes the thing that is wrong with society is not the responsibility of any one person. Environmentalists cannot point to one person or company that caused all environmental damage. Feminists cannot point to one source for all misogyny. That does not mean that nothing can be done, but rather that promoting justice is the task of everybody. But when we are aware of injustice all around us, of wrongness all around us, we can sometimes look for scapegoats on whom to focus our righteous anger. Misogyny is widespread, but this misogynist in particular needs to be made an example of. Racial prejudice is widespread, but this example in particular needs to be denounced strongly.

This is sometimes called "virtue signaling," when someone publicly mirrors in word or symbolic gesture what important segments of the people are feeling. If the people are angry, I show them that I'm angry too. Sometimes the virtue signaling comes from a protective instinct, trying to avoid the anger of the mob. (Do not look at me; I'm angry too!) Sometimes it comes from a desire to capitalize on the momentum of a particular feeling. (I'm angry too! Read my website! Donate to my nonprofit! Support my campaign!) Virtue signaling rarely allows for nuance.

With the advent of social media, denouncing often takes the form of a virtual mob, as people share and forward and reblog not just the latest instance of injustice but also the name and address and social security number of the perpetrator so that an example can be made.

"The Wrath of a Man Does Not Accomplish the Righteousness of God"

A few centuries after Aristotle defended righteous anger, the Roman Stoic philosopher Seneca pointed out a problem with it. Philosophy, he argued, is supposed to make us wise, make us better people, and certainly distinguish us from mindless beasts or crazy people. Well, Seneca observed, there is a lot of injustice in the world. Injustice is so pervasive, in fact, that even if we followed Aristotle's advice to have just the right amount of anger toward every injustice we learn about, we would be angry all the time, and (according to the theory) correctly so. We would be angry at racism and sexism, at religious discrimination and wasteful government spending, at conspicuous consumption on the personal level and the exploitation of the worker, at environmental degradation and cruelty to animals, at the plight of refugees, and at domestic violence and sex trafficking and child abuse and on and on. If we were to live this way, we would be so angry at so many things that there would hardly be a difference between our supposedly virtuous selves and a raving lunatic. We would become bitter. Therefore, it seems unlikely that anger, even righteous anger, is actually a good thing.

Scripture largely agrees with Seneca's critique of anger. Saint James tells us in his epistle, "The wrath of a man does not accomplish the righteousness of God" (1:20). "Refrain from anger; abandon wrath; do not be provoked; it brings only harm," warns the psalmist (Ps 37:8). Saint Paul condemns anger: "But now you must put them all away: anger, fury, malice, slander, and obscene language out of your mouths" (Col 3:8). In the Sermon on the Mount, Jesus forbids anger in the strongest terms: "I say to you, whoever is angry with his brother will be liable to judgment, and whoever says to his brother, 'Raqa,' will be answerable to the Sanhedrin, and whoever says, 'You fool,' will be liable to fiery Gehenna" (Mt 5:22).

People assume that Jesus must have been angry while flipping over the money changers' tables in the Temple, but in fact that is described as a result of his "zeal" (Jn 2:17), not his anger. Nobody who saw Jesus do this thought he was losing it; they interpreted it rather as a sign (Jn 2:23), especially since, afterward, he sat down and taught the people about the meaning of what he did (Mk 11:17). There is one example in the Gospels where Jesus is described as angry, in Mark 3:5, when he is about to heal a man's withered hand on the sabbath: "Looking around at [those in the synagogue] with anger and grieved at their hardness of heart, he said to the man, 'Stretch out your hand.' He stretched it out and his hand was restored." The word for "anger" used here, *orge*, is used elsewhere in the New Testament to refer mainly to God's settled disposition to punish, especially at the end of time.

Anger is associated with the devil both by Saint Paul ("Do not let the sun set on your anger, and do not leave room for the devil" [Eph 4:26–27]) and in the story of Cain, where anger opens the door to the devil and to murder: "Cain was very angry and dejected. Then the LORD said to Cain: Why are you angry? Why are you dejected? If you act rightly, you will be accepted; but if not, sin lies in wait at the door: its urge is for you, yet you can rule over it" (Gen 4:5–7). As a result of this scriptural hint, many Desert Fathers thought that anger came from demonic temptation. Evagrius Ponticus writes about a demon of anger, one of whose principal goals was to distract the saints during their prayer. I certainly find it true that if, during a time of prayer, I find myself remembering something that makes me angry, I tend to revisit it and pick at it and obsess over it, all of which does make it hard to focus on God for the rest of my prayer time.

Anger, especially righteous anger, can easily drive out charity and mercy. If we get angry about justice, especially if we are sure we are in the right, we can easily become angry at the people who fall short of justice. Seneca points out that this would only make sense if the world were not fallen, if human imperfection were a rare thing, rather than (what is actually the case) that human *excellence* is a rare thing.

If it is to be expected that most people are failures, trapped in their passions and sins, one should not react with surprise and anger. The virtuous man manages his expectations. He approaches sinners as a doctor does his patients, seeing whether there is something one can do to make things better—or as a ship's captain approaches a leak by just fixing it (rather than pointlessly getting angry). Mercy, working to right what is wrong, is the only rational response.

Equity and Mercy in the Service of a Humane Personalism

In the early 1990s, the liberal and feminist philosopher Martha Nussbaum criticized the tendency for radical politics to

promote justice without equity or mercy.[1] Her target was
the radical feminist Andrea Dworkin, but her point could be
expanded to much of our political life today. Our thirst for
justice can often become too abstract, she argued, so that in
our fight against pervasive injustice we can lose track of the
concrete details of individual people's stories. When we scapegoat someone for his role in a larger injustice, when we make
an example of somebody, we do not care about treating the
scapegoat justly.

Justice is not just about universal laws but also about particular people with particular histories and faults who make
particular decisions under particular circumstances, and often
those personal stories help to explain and contextualize the
decisions that are being denounced. Police brutality is a general problem, but the details of *this* case exonerate *this* police
officer—despite the protestors outside the courthouse who
want an example made of him. In classical times, this form of
particularized justice was called "equity."

A student of mine complained about a family gathering
with an elderly uncle who has lots of opinions about politics,
opinions that the student believed were racist. "How can I
put up with all those terrible ideas?" asked the student. "As
a Catholic, am I not obliged to denounce injustice wherever
I see it?" "Well," I asked, "can you tell a story about your
uncle that helps explain these views? You love him as part of
the family, do you not? Can you tap into that love to try to
understand why he says these things? Might he be repeating
political opinions that he hears on television without seeing
all the implications that you do? Are these ideas the most
important thing in your relationship? Do you really believe
he is an imminent threat to society? Can you strengthen your
relationship in nonpolitical areas (for example, talk about his

---

1   Martha C. Nussbaum, "Equity and Mercy," *Philosophy and Public Affairs* 22 (1993): 83–125.

favorite sports team or novel), and once when your relationship is stronger, then maybe you can talk about politics?" The student was making the mistake, typical of those who care a lot about justice, of seeing the uncle solely as a promoter of injustice. My goal was to situate the uncle's political views in the context of the life story of a person with whom the student had a personal relationship characterized by familial bonds. A concern for equity forces us to think that way, to consider the person as well as the injustice, the sinner as well as the sin. And it can help deal with righteous anger.

Equity is an important aspect of justice, and yet, Nussbaum points out, it is not the same as mercy. That is, even if we had a perfectly equitable and particularized determination of what is just in this person's case, we still have options about what to do in the future. We might decide to give the person another chance, or bear with his faults, or decide that the lesson has already been learned and the person is not a threat to society. The Twitter mob, already angry at one flavor or another of widespread injustice, might not be satisfied; but that is partly because they only have a concept of justice in their politics, and justice without a concern for individual people, argues Nussbaum, is inhumane.

Every concept of justice must have a humane strategy for dealing with cases where things go wrong; our political discourse today too often does not. When our politics focus only on justice, our political life becomes unrealistic. We lose track of the stories, the motivations, the struggles, and the moral triumphs of the people who live around us. Our expectations for people are unrealistic. We become naive about sin at the same time that we are enraged about injustice. Rather than justice leading us to a better society, it leads us to one where we cannot get along with one another. Without an understanding of mercy, our society will eventually become unstable.

Liberal Tolerance and Justice-Only Politics

You might think that our political life has an easy response to this: tolerance. If we stop being so judgmental about people, then we can all get along. Liberal democracies have evolved so as to let us live together in pluralistic societies, where we can disagree in organized ways through parliaments and elections. All we have to do is to respect people's rights and be tolerant, and our politics will be stable.

I am skeptical about this. The word "tolerance" actually refers to two different ideas, only one of which is helpful. The word comes from the Latin *tolerare*, meaning to bear, endure, support, sustain, or suffer, and traditionally to tolerate or bear with others' faults was considered one of the spiritual works of mercy. A related spiritual work of mercy was admonishing or correcting sinners. We will talk more about the works of mercy in a later chapter, but clearly both bearing with others' faults and correcting sinners are compatible with each other, since they are both works of mercy.

A key feature of political tolerance in today's liberal state is that we are not allowed to correct other people about their choices, so long as they respect the rights of others. Liberal tolerance today urges us to accept the other person and not to judge people for doing what they think is right (judgmentalism is a sin related to intolerance). Those who are judgmental—it is often said—are intolerant, and (paradoxically) cannot be tolerated.

Mercy implies solidarity with the person to whom one shows mercy; the corporal and spiritual works of mercy require us to care about the bodies and souls of others. Liberal tolerance requires its practitioners not to care about the souls of others in society, in the name of not having arguments about right and wrong and promoting social peace. But accepting people as they are can imply that "how they are" is not in any way wrong. (In any case, who are you to judge?)

You can tell whether people mean merciful tolerance or liberal tolerance by whether they worry about *intolerance*. Intolerance is not usually a problem for the work of mercy—you cannot really get righteously angry at someone for not bearing with your faults. But intolerance for a liberal is effectively a threat against peace and justice, and so a threat to society. It makes complete sense to be angry at those who threaten the stability of our society.

Liberalism promotes itself as a way of life that allows people from different backgrounds and with different ways of life to live together in peace. Yet the most perceptive liberals admit that there is a limit to what liberalism can tolerate. The famous philosopher of liberalism John Rawls has argued that it would be a threat to the peace and stability of society if there were anyone who thought that there was some good higher than politics that all people ought to pursue. He mentions as examples of such intolerant people Thomas Aquinas, Ignatius of Loyola, and the Protestant Reformers and describes them as having a sort of insanity: "It strikes us as irrational, or more likely as mad," to "subordinate all our aims to one end," such as following the will of God.[2] The liberal philosopher Richard Rorty expressed this line of thinking vividly:

> We heirs of the Enlightenment think of enemies of liberal democracy like Nietzsche or Loyola as, to use Rawls's word, "mad." We do so because there is no way to see them as fellow citizens of our constitutional democracy, people whose life plans might, given ingenuity and good will, be fitted in with

---

2   Rawls describes Saint Ignatius of Loyola and Saint Thomas Aquinas as examples of those who advocate loving and serving God as man's dominant end. Summarizing Ignatius' *Spiritual Exercises*, Rawls writes, "Furthering the divine intentions is the sole criterion for balancing subordinate aims. It is for this reason alone that we should prefer health to sickness, riches to poverty, honor to dishonor, a long life to a short one.... We must be ... ready to take the course that we believe is most for the glory of God." Rawls then criticizes such views: "It strikes us as irrational, or more likely as mad," to "subordinate all our aims to one end." *A Theory of Justice* (Cambridge, MA: Belknap Press of Harvard University Press, 1999), §83, 485–86. For the Protestant Reformers, see §§34–35, 189–94.

those of other citizens.... They are crazy because the limits of sanity are set by what we can take seriously. This, in turn, is determined by our upbringing, our historical situation.[3]

If intolerant people—including those who seek to organize their whole lives around obedience to God's will—ever became too numerous or influential, argue these extremely influential political philosophers, well, then liberal democracies would have to suppress them. Such people's influence and ideas, Rawls writes, "should be contained, like war or disease."[4]

It is not just religious people whom liberal tolerance cannot tolerate, nor does tolerance present a challenge to all religious people. There can be liberal and tolerant religious people, who keep their religious views to themselves, who do not try to change the world according to their religious views, who refuse to apply their standards of right and wrong to the behavior of others. And there can be intolerant nonreligious people, those who think that their view of environmental or racial or feminist justice is so important that society should be organized around it, that everyone should adopt it, and that those who do not are immoral and should be punished. They believe that social peace is less important than doing what is right, that in principle it is acceptable to violate individual rights in the name of a higher justice. The theory of liberalism opposes anyone who has an overarching view of what is good and right that does not allow the personal and political to be cordoned off from each other. Any such people are a threat to liberal social peace, and peace is the highest political goal.

The irony here is that in the name of preventing one set of social conflicts, tolerant liberalism threatens to provoke

---

3   Richard Rorty, "The Priority of Democracy to Philosophy," in *Objectivity, Relativism, and Truth* (Cambridge: Cambridge University Press, 1991), 187–88.

4   John Rawls, *Political Liberalism* (New York: Columbia University Press, 1996), 64n19; cf. Rawls, *Theory of Justice*, §34–35, 189–94.

another. Tolerance is not mercy but rather is a part of liberal conceptions of justice. Which means that, perhaps surprisingly, today's tolerant liberalism is another form of what we have called justice-only politics. And like all justice-only politics, it can be inhumane toward those who oppose it and can lead to conflict and social instability over time.

5

Solidarity and Mercy

The practice of scapegoating, even when done in the name of "justice," tends to lead to division in society, as we "throw people under the bus" and "kick them to the curb," anathematizing them for their past behavior contrary to impersonal justice. If our idea of justice is abstract enough, it might be that no real person is actually able to achieve it all the time, and so in their merciless scrutiny the watchdogs of "justice" threaten everybody. Justice-only politics aspires to totalitarian tyranny.

It was against the background of such worries that ancient political thinkers came to realize that mercy was needed as a stabilizing force in politics. The ancient Stoic Seneca pointed out that the tyrants of history usually had shorter reigns than those known for clemency, in part because having a reputation for mercy leads people to like you, and gaining the love of a populace leads to greater stability than relying on their fear to obey you. And of course, if they love you, they are less likely to overthrow you. A ruler without mercy would react strongly to the slightest failure or insult, while a clement ruler would let lesser offenses slide. A clement ruler seeks alliances and friends and punishes only reluctantly, while a merciless ruler punishes easily and has only subordinates and enemies, and the subordinates he uses to control his enemies are all potential enemies.

In a powerful passage, Seneca contrasts the tyrant who governs by fear and is afraid of everyone with the king "whose care embraces all":

> [The king], while guarding here with greater vigilance, there with less, yet fosters each and every part of the state as a portion of himself; who is inclined to the milder course even if it would profit him to punish, showing thus how loath he is to turn his hand to harsh correction; whose mind is free from all hostility, from all brutality; who so covets the approbation of his countryman upon his acts as ruler that he wields his power with mildness and for their good; who thinks himself aboundingly happy if he can make the public sharers in his own good fortune; who is affable in speech, accessible, loveable ... well-disposed to just petitions and even to the unjust is not harsh—such a one the whole state loves, defends, and reveres. What people say of such a man is the same in secret as in public.... Such a prince, protected by his own good deeds, needs no bodyguard; the arms he wears are for adornment only. (*De Clementia* 1.13.4ff.)[1]

Mercy here leads the king to solidarity with the people, in which the king regards his realm as a part of himself and acts for the good of his people as his own good, and the people reciprocate by trusting him and defending him and loving him back. In a subsequent passage, Seneca calls the king "the father of his country" and says that his exercise of punishment has the character of a father disciplining his son, correcting his bad behavior out of a love for what he could be, and only disinheriting him "when great and repeated wrongdoing has overcome his patience, only when what he fears outweighs what he reprimands" (1.14).

---

1   Excerpt from *Seneca: Moral Essays*, vol. 1, *De Providentia. De Constantia. De Ira. De Clementia*, trans. John W. Basore, Loeb Classical Library (Cambridge, MA: Harvard University Press, 1928, reprinted 1998), 397–99.

The biblical king David is portrayed as an example of a king who governed in this generous way. He felt pain when his people were punished by a plague for his own pride, asking God to let him be punished rather than his people (2 Sam 24:10–17). He put up with the insults of Shimei the Benjamite when his men wanted to avenge the insults (2 Sam 16:5–14). He refused to retaliate when King Saul attacked him, but on multiple occasions he responded to threats with loyalty and offers of peace (1 Sam 24; 26). When someone did kill Saul and thought he would be happy, he was instead upset (2 Sam 1:11). His son Absalom nearly defeated him in a coup, but David never wavered in his paternal love for him or desired his death even when his life was in danger. He desired friendship with his enemies, showed solidarity with his people, and tolerated those who insulted him. And, as Seneca observed, David had a long reign and his son peacefully inherited his realm.

Fear, Love, and Solidarity

Seneca makes a strong case that reciprocal love between a populace and its government creates a more stable regime than subservient fear. Not everyone has agreed with him. Machiavelli famously thought that political fear provided greater stability than political love. Fear, he observed, appealed to people's self-interest, while love required them to be virtuous and transcend their self-interest. According to Machiavelli, since everyone is naturally self-interested, a society that ignores virtue and depends on people acting in their self-interest is built on a more stable foundation.

Today, however, a version of Seneca's idea has made a comeback in political theory. The Harvard philosopher John Rawls, whom we met in the last chapter, was a significant figure in twentieth-century political thought. Rawls convincingly argued that the political stability of a society is greatly increased if people *believe in the principles* on which the society is based, and greatly decreased if they do not agree with the principles but rather obey the laws simply out of fear of punishment.

Machiavelli and Seneca both focused on the people's attitude toward this or that particular king or emperor. In a modern democracy with checks and balances on executive power, however, the important question is not whether we love or fear the person who happens to be president of our country, since that person will change eventually. The more important question is whether we actively support the basic principles and structures of our society. If we agree with the principles of society, then we will want to help society to live up to its principles, and so we will work to support the laws and goals of society. Good people will make the effort to run for office and, motivated by public ideals, will serve in important social roles. The more people there are who agree that a society is good and just, the stronger the society will be.

If, however, we did not care about the principles of our society, if we thought its goals were rotten, then we would not make the effort to build it up or maintain it. We would likely do only the minimum it took to be left alone to live our lives without interference. And if it stopped being worth it to support the current arrangement of society, we might opt for change, even if that meant supporting a revolution or a coup.

Communism and Solidarity

The end of Communism provided an interesting test case for this debate about love versus fear in governing. Because neither Lenin nor Stalin nor their henchmen operated with a sense of mercy for those who fell short of Communist ideals, the Soviet Union and its client states in Eastern Europe were largely governed through fear of punishment. Communism in theory was about creating a just society, but because it lacked an operative concept of mercy, any slight deviation from what the Communist Party taught to be right behavior or right thinking could lead to a trial, imprisonment, exile, or execution—all in the name of justice. Striving for justice without a humane plan for what to do when people fell short of it or disagreed with those ideals led to severity in government and a fearful populace.

In Poland, John Paul II and Lech Wałęsa started a movement called Solidarity (in Polish, *Solidarność*), named after the virtue that rejects the idea that we are all isolated individuals and instead strives to create interpersonal bonds through which we support one another because we are on the same side. Solidarity is closely related to mercy; part of mercy is to make it our personal concern to help the person in need. We found this virtue described in the passage from Seneca quoted above (although Seneca called it *humanitas*, from which we get "humanitarian" and "humane"). The king who regards the good of his people as his own personal good, who acts toward his people as a father toward his children, demonstrates solidarity. He is on the side of the people; he cares for them, and even his disciplinary actions are done with a paternal concern.

Importantly, solidarity is often an antidote to fear; if in this life we all band together, then we each individually have less to fear. There is a certain point beyond which, if enough people are on the same side, punishment is not really an option—you cannot punish everybody or almost everybody.

By promoting solidarity and reducing the fear of punishment, the Polish people attacked the Communist regime at what Seneca and Rawls (but not Machiavelli) would have regarded as its weakest point: its reliance on fear to govern.

They faced the soldiers and politicians and asked them: Why can't we live a better way than this? Why invest ourselves in this awful way of living? Why shoot us just for wanting more? Starting in 1989, first in Poland, then in Hungary, and then throughout the majority of the Soviet bloc, soldiers and others who worked for the governments decided to stop governing through fear. And then on Christmas Day 1991, the Soviet Union dissolved itself. The regime of uncompromising revolutionary ideals about a just society found that aiming for justice while being merciless led to instability and its downfall.

Mercy = Solidarity with the Needy + the Power to Make a Difference

Mercy is more than just solidarity; it is solidarity that *restores* and *corrects*. As we saw earlier, if mercy is the ability to make something better, then to be merciful you must also be powerful. It is not enough to want to do something—you must be able to make a difference. You cannot be suffering from the same problem you are trying to remedy. You cannot help the poor if you do not have any money to give; you cannot bury the dead unless you are alive. The ability to provide what the other person needs implies that, in the relevant sense, you are strong enough to help. That is the basis of your superiority over the person you want to help—not that you are better in every sense, but in the relevant sense that you can actually do something.

Sometimes our solidarity today means we need to acquire more power than we have, so as to be in a position to be merciful tomorrow. You cannot feed the hungry unless you can get some food; if you are poor yourself and you want to help those in need, you need to find money.

That means mercy is inescapably about power, about getting it and about using it to help those in need out of a sense of solidarity. That might make some people nervous. Is that not the plot of about half the science-fiction movies, in which a scientist becomes a mad scientist in his quest for more and more power to do the most good? Does not that suggest that mercy could be dangerous, that people might be corrupted out of a desire to do good? Not necessarily.

Mercy Makes Inequality Benign

"Inequality" is almost a four-letter word in politics today, something that we need to eliminate or reduce. In certain circles, "inequality" is a synonym for social evil. For example, the Organisation for Economic Co-operation and Development (OECD), an influential nongovernmental organization (NGO), declares that reducing inequality is simply identical to progress across a host of areas.

But if you examine this claim more closely, it becomes clear that their real concerns are with a host of other problems for which inequality is seen as a cause. Inequality creates social divisions, a lack of self-esteem among the marginalized groups, a sense that they do not fully belong to society, and a perception that society is stacked against them. On its webpage entitled "Inclusive Growth," the OECD website states, "People would feel more motivated and involved if the benefits of economic growth were not allowed to flow into the pockets of a rich minority.... With the right policies and investments in essential public services, we can build more cohesive societies and bridge the divides that threaten our future prosperity." Fighting inequality is here perceived as a means to the end of greater social cohesion, or, to put it another way, to greater solidarity.

This suggests that the complaint of the OECD and others who see inequality as a problem could be solved if the inequality did not lead to greater social divisions but rather to greater solidarity.

How is this possible? Well, mercy is the virtue that makes one person's superior power relative to another *benign*, a force for solidarity and mutual support rather than domination, exploitation, or indifference. A merciful person sees one's power with respect to another as the ability to help. Yes, such power can corrupt or lead the rich and powerful to regard others as lesser people, but (as Seneca argued) mercy is the virtue that fights against such tendencies.

Works of Mercy Can Unite the Strong and the Weak

In the tradition of the Church, equality has never really been a goal, but solidarity with those less fortunate is an essential requirement of salvation. In the account of the Last Judgment (Mt 25:31–46), Jesus condemns to eternal punishment all those who fail to show solidarity to the needy. Saint Paul says, "Have the same regard for one another; do not be haughty but associate with the lowly" (Rom 12:16). The Church Fathers preached fiery sermons against the rich hoarding their wealth and praised those who gave generously to the needy.

The chief way of uniting the powerful and the powerless has been through almsgiving. Since Saint Thomas places all the traditional works of mercy under the category of almsgiving, we can see that it unites the rich and the poor, the educated and the uneducated, the strong and the weak, even the living and the dead. Almsgiving begins with inequality and yet produces solidarity.

In addition to the many, many saints who gave away their riches in order to enter religious life, the Church has recognized extremely wealthy laypeople—including aristocrats, kings, and queens—for their almsgiving and acts of solidarity with the poor: Saint Louis IX of France, Saint Stephen of Hungary, Saint Casimir, Blessed Pier Giorgio Frassati, Saints Elizabeth and Margaret of Hungary, Saint Elizabeth of Portugal, and Saint Margaret of Scotland, among others. Saint Charles Borromeo famously spent all his family's great wealth during a famine in an attempt to feed sixty thousand people daily. Saint Vincent de Paul organized wealthy women to support his work with the poor.

We can think of one example from our experience. In our current tax code, we refer to a certain class of organizations as "charitable." In English law a few centuries back, these organizations were instead called "eleemosynary," from the Greek word *eleemosyne*, which means "mercy" (it shares the same root as the Kyrie Eleison in the Mass), rather than the Latin word for love (*caritas*). The English word "alms" seems to be a corrupted pronunciation of *eleemosyne* (and while "corrupted pronunciation" sounds judgmental, I do not really blame anyone for it—*eleemosyne* is quite a mouthful to say). All of which is to say that what we tend to call charitable works today used to be called works of mercy and are related to almsgiving.

If we think about our tax-deductible charities today, they do not merely include soup kitchens and homeless shelters but also universities. That is an unusual grouping in our culture—universities seem to be places for the elites, not places for the wretched. But when we take into account the medieval Christian background of a lot of our laws, we can see that both are works of mercy, educating the ignorant just as much as feeding the hungry. Why do we give tax breaks to this class of institutions? Because we want to encourage those with money to donate to them, because we know that few works for the poor will flourish without the patronage of the wealthy. Even today, therefore, we can recognize that inequality is not necessarily a barrier to solidarity, so long as those who are more powerful act with mercy for the benefit of those in need. Works of mercy can increase social cohesion even across social divisions.

Mercy Must Be Ordered toward the Common Good

It is certainly possible to help others in a way that makes other things worse. It is a common complaint of the computer programmers I minister to at MIT that when they try to fix one part of their code, they end up breaking another part. If you are assembling furniture from IKEA, you usually cannot tighten only one screw all the way down, or else you cannot get all the other parts to fit into place. The same thing goes with people. We can fix one social problem but create another. We can give money to a beggar and contribute to his drug habit. We can develop high-tech prostheses for amputees and help Darth Vader build an evil Galactic Empire. Our desire to cure diseases can tempt us to use unethical research methods.

This is also true for our almsgiving. Our charity can create dependencies or disrupt local economies. An American shoe company ships a load of free shoes to a developing country, and the temporary influx of free, superior products drives local shoemakers out of business. The award-winning 2014 documentary *Poverty, Inc.* argues that foreign aid to Third World countries often ruins local economies and perpetuates poverty rather than reduces it.

The poor will always be with us, says our Lord (Jn 12:8), and no amount of goodwill and human effort will solve all the problems we find in this fallen world. To think otherwise is the heresy of Pelagianism, the idea that we did not need Jesus' death to save us, that our human efforts can be enough to fix our broken humanity. The world will remain fallen and broken and imperfect until the Second Coming.

That does not mean that we do not try to help people who need help or that doing so is pointless. The Second Vatican Council's Pastoral Constitution on the Church in the Modern World, *Gaudium et Spes* (December 7, 1965), taught that "while earthly progress must be carefully distinguished from the growth of Christ's kingdom, to the extent that the former can contribute to the better ordering of human society, it is of vital concern to the Kingdom of God" (39). But it does mean that we need to exercise mercy prudently, using good judgment so that in "debugging" one part of society we do not unintentionally break another part.

This gets to a deep point: mercy must be ordered toward justice; it must be in the service of overall good order. Our attempts to help others actually have to help, not just in the narrow way that we have conceived it but in a way that promotes the common good.

6

Punishment without Solidarity or Mercy

For decades before social networking, we did not have a lot of angry mobs in America. Now that we have virtual mobs destroying a person's reputation, we can appreciate why they are not great for social order. Mobs get emotional and sometimes get carried away when they think someone has done something wrong. They act irrationally and arbitrarily. They can dehumanize their scapegoats, demanding excessively harsh treatment. They can attack the wrong person and judge rashly. Most societies try to limit and control mobs in the name of reason and justice and good social order. That is partly why the institution of punishment developed: to sideline the angry mob. Punishment involves a tremendous moral responsibility because it involves the exercise of great power over the lives of those being punished. If it is to be an improvement over the mob, it must be humane to the prisoner, and it must deal with evil and injustice and disorder in a way that promotes the common good.

Philosophers have long realized that punishment is a complex human activity. Most thinkers seem to agree that the practice of punishment accomplishes each of the following at least some of the time: incapacitating the offender from committing future crimes; deterring others by making the costs of crime outweigh the benefits; keeping public order; denouncing the offender's actions; reforming the offender so as to be a law-abiding citizen; teaching the offender that what he did was wrong; restoring trust within the community; reconciling the offender with society; and righting past wrongs.

In order to punish well, we have to answer the questions of who, what, how much, and why. There is a fair amount of consensus about the first question: we should punish only those who are guilty. But on the other questions, especially the last, smart and good people disagree strongly. There is considerable agreement that punishment accomplishes (more or less) all of these purposes; the debate is over which of these should predominate.

Retribution as a Theory of Punishment

For some people, retribution is the primary moral purpose of punishment. The word "retribution" comes from the Latin word meaning "to give back" (*tribuere* means "to give," as in the English word "tribute"). The basic idea of retribution is derived from the meaning of the word: that one who has sinned in the past must be made to "give back" what it was that he took in sinning. As a theory of why we punish, retribution has several characteristics:

- It is backward looking, focusing on the past wrong.
- It is proportional, seeking to make the punishment fit the crime, as in "an eye for an eye."
- It is focused solely on the question of guilt rather than on the moral improvement of the offender, the deterrence of future crimes, or the good order of the society.
- It aims at restoring the equilibrium of an earlier status quo, which the offender's action has destabilized.
- It conceives of punishing as a duty, that it is morally necessary to take from the offender what he took undeservedly so that things are made right again.

Immanuel Kant, one of the most influential philosophers of the last several centuries, was one of the foremost thinkers to hold that retribution is the purpose of punishment (rather than one consideration among others). He held that retribution was always a duty, that no punishment could ever be set aside, even if a greater good could be served (say, by getting a lesser criminal to turn on his boss). Otherwise, the social equilibrium could not be restored.[1]

Retribution and Vengeance

Retribution is not the same as vengeance or anger, as it is sometimes thought to be. It is actually supposed to be rather calculating and unemotional. You took from society or the common good, and now you have to give back what you took or its equivalent. The requirement that punishment be "proportionate" to the crime sounds almost mathematically precise. That is both a strength and a weakness. Retribution rules out over-the-top, cruel, and unusual punishments, since those would not be proportionate to the crime. When Hammurabi came up with the policy of "an eye for an eye," it was meant to use proportionality as an upper limit of punishment, as a way of preventing the escalation of violence and putting a limit on the harsh treatment of offenders. An eye for an eye and no more.

That punishment should be proportionate to the crime is, however, merely a starting point. In many situations of real life,

---

1   A classic example of Kant's pure retributivist position is found in this passage: "Even if a civil society were to be dissolved by the consent of all its members (e.g., if a people inhabiting an island decided to separate and disperse throughout the world), the last murderer remaining in prison would first have to be executed, so that each has done to him what his deeds deserve and blood guilt does not cling to the people for not having insisted on his punishment; for otherwise the people can be regarded as collaborators in this [the murderer's] public violation of justice." Immanuel Kant, *The Metaphysics of Morals* (Berlin: Royal Prussian Academy of the Sciences, 1902), 331–33.

after all, it is difficult to find punishments that are proportionate to the crime. And that means that it is not always possible to make the offender "give back" what he "took" in committing a crime. What is the equal and opposite reaction to bigamy? To calumny? To the murder of a promising young doctor in the bloom of youth by a desperate junkie with two months to live? Certainly, there are many crimes where the punishment can be meted out in a rough equivalence to the crime: a thief can be required to give back what he stole, or a vandal who has spray-painted rude graffiti all over a public monument can be made to clean it up. Nevertheless, it seems clear that an adequate theory of punishment must be informed by a richer sense of the end of punishment.

This conclusion becomes clearer when we consider the occasions in which, for the greater order, we do not punish retributively. We do this every time we give a criminal immunity or witness protection in exchange for testimony against his crime boss. If the idea of retribution were followed strictly, then it would be a moral *duty* to punish a low-level criminal in a manner that fits the crime, no matter how counterproductive that would be for society. If we were to insist upon a quasi-mathematical ideal of retribution, we might end by regarding mercy as immoral. Any deviation from the punishment strictly proportionate to the crime would leave society in disequilibrium. A wrong would not have been righted. The offender who took something from society would not have had to give it back. A debt would still need to be paid.

Deterrence, Fear, and Cost-Benefit Analysis

Another common approach to punishment is to think that it is best understood by its deterrence value. The idea that punishment is supposed to deter future crime is in some sense the opposite of the retributive idea. Where retribution was primarily backward looking, deterrence is entirely forward looking. In addition to being forward looking, deterrence can also help society heal by denouncing the injustice publicly and in the strongest terms. The harsher the punishment, the more clearly society disapproves of the evil.

Deterrence tries to use fear of punishment to control crime and influence behavior. Modern political thinkers have tried to develop defenses of governing by fear that could allow governments to deter crime without being tyrannical. Perhaps the earliest sophisticated argument that deterrence should be the main aim of punishment came from the eighteenth-century English theorist Jeremy Bentham. One of the first utilitarians, Bentham claimed that most human reasoning could be explained as a form of cost-benefit analysis. Having a publicly known list of punishments, he argued, helped people accurately to analyze the costs of breaking the law, and therefore (if the system of punishments were properly calibrated) would incentivize most people to obey the law. Criminals who thought they could skirt the law were educated through the pains of punishment that they were wrong, and so they learned that "crime does not pay."

Some deterrence theorists have argued that it is always better to have harsher and harsher penalties so that the costs of crime vastly outweigh the benefits and criminals are thus more strongly deterred. Prisons should not be too comfortable, but should be unpleasant places where overcrowding, bad food, and threats from other prisoners add to the punitive character of the experience. Making prisons unpleasant places makes crime less attractive, and the more unpleasant, the less attractive crime becomes. Bentham disagreed. He argued that punishments should not be any heavier than necessary, since punishing has costs to society. Prisons are expensive in financial terms and in human terms, since prisoners do not contribute to their families or to society. Overpunishing costs too much for the benefits it brings. We see this in our time when, after decades of longer sentences for a wider variety of crimes, our prisons are overcrowded and we have either to let out people who have not yet shown they are ready or to build more prisons.

Deterrence Frustrates Solidarity

The attractiveness of deterrence approaches comes largely from their concern for a version of the common good. Although pessimistic and lacking a rich idea of justice, their moral psychology, which regards individuals as self-interested and calculating, is not completely wrong. Through virtue and grace, we can become more than self-interested, but we are always at least somewhat self-interested so long as we experience reality in the first person.

That utilitarian moral psychology, however, also reveals a weakness of deterrence approaches to punishment. Because they do not aspire to teach anything more than rational self-interest, they do not increase loyalty to society or support for its institutions. They have no ambition to teach either society or the offender to care about solidarity, justice, or the common good. As we saw earlier in the case of Communist Poland, a society in which people are governed by fear of punishment is less stable than one in which people believe in its principles. If everyone is taught to obey the law or else be punished, but not to see society as something important to serve and support, people will stop working to make society stronger. A utilitarian society is little more than a bunch of self-serving individuals living in proximity. Its order is imposed from without by the threat of punishment, and if ever the costs of criminality decline, if ever the authorities waver in their attention or their resolve to punish, people might recalculate and decide it is actually rational to break the law.

Deterrence approaches to punishment are often criticized for another problem: while they care about society, they do not care about the prisoner. They are concerned with the offender only insofar as he serves as an example for others, and they do not treat him with dignity or as an end in himself. Moreover, if we are concerned only with the deterrence value of punishing, it does not really matter whether the person punished is even guilty of the crime, so long as the public believes so. If done skillfully, scapegoating would be just as helpful for public order as punishing the guilty, or perhaps more so; a show trial teaches its lessons clearly, while a real trial might confuse the public lesson with messy facts.

Imagine the following scenario (from the nightmares of this Boston priest). If a lawyer calls a press conference announcing that he has the name of a priest abuser that the diocese has not made public, the media will hound the bishop for days. If the bishop uses internal administrative procedures to remove the priest from ministry permanently and makes that fact public, the media will stop harassing him, and the public will know that the bishop is strongly against abuse. If instead he holds a canonical trial and there is not enough evidence to convict the priest, people might accuse the bishop of being soft on abuse or not trusting the accusers. The Church's credibility is fragile because she has been soft on abuse in the past; unless the priest is removed, the public will assume that she is being soft in this case also. A cost-benefit analysis could conclude that the common good of the diocese is thus better served by settling with the lawyer and scapegoating an innocent priest than by risking the public blowback that could come from going through a balanced investigation and trial.

What Fear of Punishment Can Do

We can see the strengths and limits of the idea that punishment has deterrence value by looking at the role the idea plays in Catholic and Jewish theology, under the name of "fear of the Lord." Those who do not think God will punish the wicked lack fear of the Lord, as we see in Psalm 10:4–6: "The wicked boast: 'God does not care; there is no God.' Yet their affairs always succeed; they ignore your judgment on high; they sneer at all who oppose them. They say in their hearts, 'We will never fall; never will we see misfortune.' " But they are wrong not to fear divine punishment, teaches Psalm 53:5–6: "Those who do evil, who feed upon my people as they feed upon bread . . . they are going to fear his name with great fear, though they had not feared it before. For God will scatter the bones of those encamped against you."

Saint Anselm of Canterbury appealed to the fear of divine punishment as that which makes it impossible for the good angels (those who did not join Satan) to sin in the future. Before Satan's fall, God had not explained that he would punish those who rebelled against him, and so Satan could entertain the idea that the benefits of sinning might outweigh the costs. Once God punished Satan, all the other angels who had remained obedient to God were now protected from being tempted: the costs of sin were so enormous—no less than eternal separation from God—that no sin could provide enough benefit, and therefore no being as smart and rational as an angel could ever find the slightest sin to be tempting.

Fear of the Lord's punishment is a gift (Is 11:2–3), a helpful reminder that obedience to God's will is in our self-interest. That is why Saint Paul exhorts us to "work out your salvation with fear and trembling," mindful that disobedience has consequences (Phil 2:12; see also Mt 10:28; Lk 1:50–51). But of course, while fear of the Lord is one of the seven gifts of the

Holy Spirit, it is not the greatest gift—that would be charity. It is okay to obey God because of fear of the loss of Heaven and the pains of Hell, but it is better to obey God because he is all-good and deserving of all our love.

Deterrence is not enough of a reason to justify a system of punishment all by itself, as Bentham and others have tried to do. But it certainly has a secondary role in punishment. It is better to obey the laws of societies because we agree with them or, at least, because we support the system of government that passed them and the ideals of the society where we live. We should aspire to that, and utilitarians are wrong not to. But if we ever were to stop being so socially conscious and start to be a little self-interested, if we were tempted to break the rules, knowing that we could be punished could help us stay in line.

Manipulation and Moral Psychology

We as individuals do not have only external behaviors but also internal motivations and reasons for our behaviors. Two people with the same exterior behavior can have different internal behaviors. One person could be a patriot, the other a spy pretending to be a patriot. One person can be a saint, the other a fraud who knows how to act piously. Jesus' warning about wolves in sheep's clothing (Mt 7:15) points out that external good behavior does not always reveal what is going on inside a person. At least not initially. Only over time, Jesus says, will interior holiness differentiate itself from false holiness: "By their fruits you will know them" (Mt 7:16). You cannot fake it forever.

We can incentivize people to behave exteriorly the way we like, at least for a time. We can bribe them with carrots or scare them with sticks. We can manipulate the amount of pleasure they gain from doing what we want and the amount of pain from doing what we do not want. But in doing so we are not treating them as true human beings. We are not trying to persuade them that what we want is good for them or for the common good; we are satisfied with their *external* compliance *for now*.

If we were lab rats who could be trained by Pavlovian methods, then manipulating our incentives might make us develop the desired habits. Since humans are a type of animal, that process works on us up to a point. But we are rational animals, which means that we choose to act according to what we have first judged to be good. A government that does not respect our thoughts and rational natures does not really treat us like men and women.

We know this about children. When the children are little, parenting can involve a fair amount of bribery and manipulation. But that does not work as the children get older and more willful. Unless the children learn self-control and how to behave morally, they will not mature. Parents have to punish in child-rearing, but the goal of that training-by-punishment is to teach and form the children so that they will flourish as adults. At least primarily. In extreme cases such as domestic abuse, a child may have to be separated from the family for reasons of self-defense. But the primary goal of the rules and punishments and other tools of raising children is that the children be persuaded to do the right thing for the right reason independently.

The differences between recalcitrant children and criminal adults are a matter of degree. Both are human beings and have the same basic human psychological capabilities. Both can fake compliance with the rules without believing in them. Both can respond to their self-interest and calculate costs and benefits. Both can be bribed or incentivized. But both can be reasoned with and perhaps persuaded to desire another way of behaving, except for those few who have truly hardened their hearts and their behavior.

The success stories of our criminal justice system are not merely about those citizens who have been deterred from ever breaking the law but also about those who after breaking the law are persuaded to become law-abiding citizens for the rest of their lives. How to achieve that good end through punishment is the focus of our next chapter.

7

Punishment with Solidarity and Mercy

In the last chapters, we have considered several theories of punishment and ways to handle injustice, all of which lack an adequate concept of mercy. In this chapter, we will look at the better way, one that cares both for each person and for the common good, one that respects the dignity of the wrongdoer while also containing the threat posed to others, one that has hope that the criminal might become a great ally for good. It also teaches us something about the way that God punishes and the reason that God punishes: for "everyone to be saved and to come to knowledge of the truth" (1 Tim 2:4).

A few chapters back we met Brother Tardy and his abbot, whose policy of leniency toward Brother Tardy led to general disorder in the monastery schedule. Let us revisit this case and ask the question, Did the abbot's decision not to discipline Brother Tardy really show mercy? Imagine if the abbot had instead thought about Brother Tardy's behavior in this way: "Brother Tardy needs to care about the other brothers. He does not see that there is a reason for the schedule, that it is not an arbitrary set of rules but that it was designed by our holy founder, Saint Benedict, to order the day toward growing in holiness. If he has a suggestion about how to change the schedule so that it better serves that purpose, I'm open to listening. But his constant lateness shows a lack of respect and love for these other men who have pledged their lives to

God in this community. If I discipline him, I will be helping him to see this, and (I hope) he will learn to love his brothers better in the practical details of our lives. I will also show all the other monks that I love them and value their time."

In this example, punishing—or, perhaps better, disciplining—someone is seen as an act of mercy. Rather than letting a disorder continue and spread, the abbot seeks to address the disordered behavior. But he is not interested merely in the external behavior. Rather, he chiefly wants Brother Tardy to understand the reason for the rules, and he wants him to regard the desired behavior (punctuality) as an act of love and respect for his brothers. If making Vespers on time is an aspect of justice in this case, then we can say he wants to teach Brother Tardy about justice and wants to convert him to desiring justice and to acting on that desire. As a result, the abbot addresses the disorder in Brother Tardy's soul, thereby helping him to become a better person while at the same time helping all the other monks by protecting the good order of the monastery. The abbot's punishment or discipline can thus be seen as helping someone who needs help, and that is clearly an act of mercy.

The word "discipline" comes from the same word as "disciple," and it implies a sort of hard coaching or tough teaching. Sometimes we have to learn things the hard way, but the hard way makes us better, as the Letter to the Hebrews reminds us: "At the time, all discipline seems a cause not for joy but for pain, yet later it brings the peaceful fruit of righteousness to those who are trained by it" (12:11). The Bible emphasizes that discipline characterizes God's fatherly love (see Heb 12:5–11; Rev 3:19; Prov 13:24). It also is a sign of his goodness and power, his ability to teach us what we need to know and train us to be how we ought to be. If we are to be merciful as our Father in Heaven is merciful, then all punishment ought to have the character of discipline in this sense, at least as much as it can in this fallen world. The *Catechism* emphasizes that punishment, "in addition to defending public order and protecting people's safety, has a medicinal purpose: as far as possible, it must contribute to the correction of the guilty party" (2266). If whenever we behaved wrongly, we could be trained and encouraged and disciplined so as to behave and think and love rightly in the future, society would be better ordered. Not only would we benefit, but the common good would benefit as well.

Justice and Mercy in the Service of Public Order

Retribution is the aspect of punishment that tries to restore society to the order it had before the crime was committed. And that is an important task, in that crime by definition is opposed to societal order, and "the desire to bring about a well-ordered society" is a serviceable definition of the virtue of justice. But the well-ordered society we aim at can be only in the future, not in the past. The past is by no means irrelevant to the future, but each day we have to start with the world as we find it and figure out how to make things better in the future. Yesterday's wrongdoing will always have happened; the crucial goal of society is that it not happen again tomorrow.

That is where mercy comes in.

As we have argued, external compliance with the rules is not enough. A society is better ordered if people support it willingly, if they agree with its principles and customs and work to support them with their own efforts. That this be the case is a key goal of justice. When talking about Communist Poland, we observed that if everyone obeys the government only because the police are everywhere, but privately they do not support it, that society is not even *stable*, let alone well-ordered. The goal of mercy is that all those who do not willingly support good order in society—in other words, all those who are opposed to justice—convert to become supporters of it. If mercy is completely successful, then society is more stable and more just because people support it wholeheartedly.

From the vantage of mercy, then, punishment has as its most important goal the leading of the criminal offender to become a law-abiding and productive member of society. To do that, the punishment must focus on changing the offender's habits—that is, his character and his convictions. Mercy tries to remove something wrong about the offender's will; the offender lacks the desire or the will to do what is right, and the work of mercy is to help elicit that desire and to help the offender persevere in it. Mercy calls us to have solidarity with wrongdoers. We always regard offenders as human beings with free will and with the possibility to reform. We want all the wrongdoers to become rightdoers. We root for them, that they both reform their behavior and have a conversion to doing good.

What Is My Responsibility?

Justice, we have argued, is about order in a society. Mercy seeks to restore that order when it has been disrupted. Before one can figure out what it means to have "good order" in a particular society, one must first determine the boundaries of the society we are trying to order. Sometimes people in business will say, "That problem is above my pay grade," by which they indicate that they do not have jurisdiction over the problem, and so it is someone else's responsibility. In order to figure out what my duties in justice are, I must determine what my sphere of responsibility is: what portion of the world I am trying to help make well-ordered. Answers can include my household, my younger sister, my department at work, my tribe, my book club, my county, the International Brother-hood of Teamsters, the Dominican Order, the soul of the penitent before me, and so on.

In order to justify vigilantism (it seems), Stan Lee, the founder and editor of Marvel Comics, put in the mouth of Peter Parker's Uncle Ben the famous "Spider-Man Moral Principle": *With power comes responsibility; with great power comes great responsibility.* Uncle Ben's dying words argue that if you have the ability to do something, you also have the responsibility to do it. There is a partial truth here. If I have a power, I should figure out how to use it responsibly. For example, if I have more spare time now that my kids are grown, I have a responsibility to use it well, and so I may volunteer to help with this year's parish festival after years of not having been able to help. If I have the money to be a philanthropist, I have a responsibility to determine how to use all that money for the common good. If I can win the election, I should think seriously about running. If I see a man lying by the side of the road to Jericho, I must decide whether to stop and help him.

The Spider-Man Principle can justify vigilantism because it shows no respect for what we just talked about—my juris-diction, my sphere of responsibility. If I can do something to help, then I must help, even if nobody in charge has given me the job to help. If I see a criminal and I can stop him, then I should stop him myself rather than wait for the police. If the United States can intervene in some international crisis, it is our responsibility to intervene, and the rest of the international community can either follow or get out of the way. The weak-ness in this principle provides one of the recurring themes in our superhero stories: if I have great power, then everything becomes my responsibility. In real life, then, in addition to figuring out what we can do, we also need to determine the boundaries of our responsibility. Sometimes the boundaries are given to us by our role or office: the legislature is supposed to write the law; the judge is supposed to apply it. Sometimes boundaries are harder to determine. People in start-up companies can find themselves doing a little of everything on the principle that if they do not do it, it will not get done.

Mercy implies that we have solidarity with everyone and therefore a disposition to help everyone; but we are not *responsible* for everyone. Thinking about this problem, the Fathers of the Church argued that our responsibility starts with the people God in his providence has placed before us. Being merciful doesn't mean we have to help everyone, just those we can reach.

I bring up the Spider-Man Principle because I think there is a corollary that is actually very important: that if I have a responsibility, I need to acquire the power to exercise it and arrive at good order. A husband who finds out he is going to be a father needs to make sure he has the income to support a larger family. If I want to help the poor, I need to find a source of money. If I want to visit those in prison, I need to have the necessary security clearances. If I want to instruct the ignorant, I need to become educated. If powerful aliens are attacking earth, we need to form the Avengers. As we have said before, mercy is solidarity plus the power to make a difference.

How to Punish with Solidarity

Step 1: Incapacitate the offender. When society is faced with an offender, someone who has already demonstrated the willingness and ability to commit crimes, the first step is usually to incapacitate the criminal, to do something that prevents him from committing the same crime right away. As we saw earlier, the Church describes this incapacitating function of punishment as a form of legitimate self-defense.

Step 2: Analyze the offender's threat to society. Once the person is incapacitated and not an immediate danger, society must decide what to do. We can maintain the person as incapacitated indefinitely or permanently, we can let him go relatively quickly (as, for instance, when his anger has cooled or he is sobered up), or we can hold him incapacitated until he shows evidence of some sort of reform. These decisions require discernment, a sort of prudential judgment about the person.

We can regard a person who committed a past crime in three ways: as a future threat to societal order, as not a threat, or as a future supporter of societal order. The future threat can be permanent or temporary, major or minor. And while criminals' past crimes will remain in the past, their behavior in the past gives us insight into their present character (which their past behaviors helped to form), and it helps predict their future behavior. If a person's character has hardened into that of a violent sociopath, for instance, we can predict that the person will be a threat to societal order in the future, and perhaps a major threat and a permanent one. A juvenile offender who let peer pressure lead him to an act of vandalism (think of Saint Augustine and the pear tree) might have a weak and malleable character and therefore might not be much of a threat in the future if he hangs out with better people. A soldier who got drunk at the death of a comrade in arms and assaulted a bartender might ordinarily be a man of good character and, absent those exact conditions, might be a force for much good in society; his crime is what we call "out of character."

If a person is judged a permanent and major threat to society, we would have to incapacitate the person permanently from committing future crimes on the grounds of legitimate self-defense.

Step 3: Try to persuade the criminal to change. In all other cases, we have reason to hope that a person can change. The moment we judge that someone is not a threat, then mercy calls us to reintegrate him into society. We have never broken solidarity; we have been rooting for the person. Now we try, step-by-step, to reduce the need for incapacitation.

As any parent who has had to discipline children knows, what works for one person does not always work for all. Some react better to yelling, some to silence or a glare, some to being grounded, some to having their phone taken away, some to a financial penalty. Sometimes it is enough to let children calm down. Other times, they are receptive to simple instruction and correction.

The same principle applies to adults. Merciful punishment, because it is pedagogical, should not be defined solely by the past crime (as in, robbery always gets two years of prison) but should include a consideration of what is likely to help discipline the criminal and improve his character. Because the goal is an improved social order going forward, our system of punishment needs the flexibility to move this person toward the goal in this way and a different person in a different way.

For example, there is a movement in criminal justice circles called "restorative justice" that tries to renew and repair the social bonds broken by crime. Much like the Truth and Reconciliation Commission in South Africa, restorative justice advocates try to bring the criminal, victim, police, and other stakeholders into a "community conference" so that those who have been affected by a crime all have the chance to face one another and repair the bonds. This sort of social healing practice markets itself as a form of justice because "mercy" is not widely perceived to be a political term. Unlike the abstract forms of justice that we criticized earlier for being divisive, restorative justice has the goal of increasing solidarity in society.

Restorative justice approaches will not always work with everyone, but they may work with some: studies have shown this sort of extrajudicial reconciliation works better than traditional punishment in the cases of juvenile delinquency and results in lower rates of recidivism (the juvenile does not return to crime). If our only goal in punishing were to treat similar cases similarly, assigning some offenders to restorative justice conferences would be unfair. But since our goal is a better-ordered society in the future, punishments should be determined by what works, what reduces recidivism, not merely by a calculation of what is supposedly fair.

Step 4: Carefully reintegrate him into society once he is no longer a threat. Think of a convicted prisoner before the state parole board. He has served a portion of his sentence, and now the board is tasked with determining whether he can safely be returned to society. The key question goes to the condition of the prisoner's intentions: Will this person be a law-abiding citizen, or will he grab the first chance he gets to go back to a life of crime? If the prisoner convinces the parole board that he respects the laws of society and even agrees with them, it is easier for the board to grant parole. If, on the other hand, he comes across as likely to obey the law only so long as the threat of punishment looms, then it is probably safer for society to keep him locked up, for it would be too hard to monitor him constantly outside the prison, and without constant monitoring he could not be trusted to obey the law. And sometimes, the board takes a calculated risk: "The prisoner seems to have learned to control his anger" (or, perhaps, "resist temptation") "in a controlled setting; can he continue to show self-control in a setting with more freedom?" In order to reduce the risk that they have misjudged the person's growth, they might use monitoring technology such as ankle bracelets or check-ins with a parole officer to reintegrate the offender gradually while at the same time giving them a way to incapacitate the person quickly if he threatens to commit another crime.

Mercy, Sentences, and Individual Discernment

The pedagogical approach to punishment that we have outlined allows for a lot of discretion on the part of the authorities. By allowing people in authority to make judgments about individuals, we give them the flexibility to balance the concerns for public safety and legitimate defense with the goal of transforming the offender into a law-abiding and productive member of society. Such an approach makes punishment more humane by taking into account the qualities of the person in question. And it can increase public order and stability, as people move from being a cost to society to being a benefit.

Some people might object to this approach for many of the reasons people object to any sort of mercy: the worry that it leads to leniency and thus disorder. It is important, therefore, to recognize that we already ask public officials to exercise their judgment all the time. At basically every level of the criminal justice system we ask officials to decide how to treat an offender. A cop must decide whether to make an arrest or to give a warning. The prosecutor must decide whether to prosecute, and then what sentence is desirable in a plea bargain or trial. The judge and perhaps jury must decide on a sentence, often within constraints by sentencing guidelines designed by the legislature. Within the prison, the warden and corrections officers make constant assessments of prisoners' attitudes toward punishment and whether they exhibit good behavior relevant to their parole status. The parole board must decide whether a convicted prisoner can safely be returned to society, and under what conditions.

The question is not whether we can eliminate the discretion of the punishing authority but how to help those who exercise judgment to do so well. A cop should not let someone off because he hates paperwork, nor should he arrest someone because he does not like people of that race. A judge should not be what they called in the old West a "hanging judge," who always convicts everybody. A parole board should seriously worry about the risk a prisoner might present. A warden should not become jaded (or overly optimistic) about the possibility of prisoner reform. And so on. Everyone who exercises discretion should keep in mind the purpose of what they do: Can they get the wrongdoer to obey the law, and do it voluntarily?

Mercy and Future Risk

It should be clear from this discussion that mercy necessarily involves some risk. If we misread a person's character or if we fool ourselves into thinking someone has reformed more than is actually the case, then society might end up less ordered than if we left the person incapacitated. Since mercy is not focused solely on the offender, but ultimately on order in society, the risk to society might constrain our ability to show mercy.

On the other hand, as we pointed out in the last chapter, there are also costs to not showing mercy. It is expensive to keep people incapacitated. Prisons are expensive in financial terms and in human terms. As of 2016, there were over 6.5 million people in the United States either in prison or in some other way subject to the criminal justice system; that is one out of every thirty-eight adults who could be involved in helping families or society but are instead simply being incapacitated.[1] To be sure, we suspect that many of them would commit further crimes if unsupervised, so there is a reason to keep them locked up for now. But if more of them changed

---

1 Danielle Kaeble and Mary Cowhig, *Correctional Populations in the United States, 2016* (U.S. Department of Justice, April 2018), 1.

their behavior, they could return to society and contribute positively. So, if we can figure out ways to maintain order and have prisoners reform, society would be better.

Criminologists today acknowledge that the crime waves of the 1970s, 1980s, and early 1990s were largely a result of bad theories of punishment. Inspired by the claims of psychiatric science to be able to "cure" prisoners' criminality through treatment programs, prisons were refashioned into rehabilitation facilities (as in the novel *A Clockwork Orange*) and prisoners were released back into society once they showed improvement. It turned out that the treatment programs had little impact on the inmates' behavior once they left prison (they weren't "cured"), and therefore the shorter sentences and early release programs were not protecting society sufficiently.[2]

In response, the "law and order" movement advocated for longer sentences and reduced discretion for judges. Among people who thought about punishment, psychiatry was discredited. Psychiatrists turned out to be bad predictors of future behavior; more importantly, their whole approach assumed that criminality was just a mental illness, which is false. Some people commit crimes out of a bad will. And sometimes punishment has to break that will before the prisoner can be trusted with freedom. There is a warning in this history: people are not always malleable. Parents know this about their children, but intellectuals sometimes ignore this truth, with disastrous consequences.

---

2   Two good histories of the failures of midcentury punishment theories can be found in John J. Dilulio Jr., *No Escape: The Future of American Corrections* (New York: Basic Books, 1991), especially the introduction, and pp. 126–47, which provide an assessment of Patuxent Institution, aka the "Clockwork Orange" prison, Maryland's experimental prison based on just such theories. Also, see Andrew von Hirsch, *Past or Future Crimes: Deservedness and Dangerousness in the Sentencing of Criminals* (New Brunswick, NJ: Rutgers University Press, 1985), especially chapter 1, "Evolution of the Debate."

8

Punishment and Mercy
in the Church Today

In the previous chapters, we have developed some ideas about how mercy can help us arrive at a more just and stable society, one that promotes the common good and social order while fostering solidarity within society and across social boundaries, and which has a humane set of responses for when people behave unjustly. The theory of merciful government and pedagogical punishment that we have explored, in which mercy isn't opposed to a justly ordered society but rather aims at it, has been in the Church for years. Some of the earliest debates in the Church were about how to reconcile those who had committed major sins such as apostasy, and the model of punishment developed then had many of the same features we explored in the last chapter. The methods of punishment and reconciliation that developed in the early Church communities later informed the types of discipline in monastic communities. The Rule of Saint Benedict has something like this theory of how to punish with charity and solidarity.

This pedagogical approach to punishment is also the way of thinking that informed how the bishops of the United States approached the crime of clergy sexual abuse of minors for the last several decades. It failed. That failure suggests either that the theory is a bad one or that there was a problem in its application. There are few analyses of the priest abuse scandal that focus on the theory of punishment at work before and after 2002; this case study is offered as an occasion to allow us to think through this tragic and difficult issue as carefully as we can.

Canon law for centuries has had ways to deal with clergy violations of the sixth commandment, but they usually involved a canonical trial and some sort of punishment. When Pope John XXIII announced that the Code of Canon Law would be revised and updated, many canon lawyers in the 1960s and afterward anticipated the direction the canonical reforms would take, encouraging the bishops not to treat clergy abuse of minors as a crime but instead as a sin and as a psychological problem that needed treatment and rehabilitation.[1] This bias against punishment and in favor of therapeutic and rehabilitative approaches was characteristic of the era, as we have seen.

It seems that diocesan policies in the 1950s and 1960s treated the sexual abuse of a minor similarly to the way dioceses dealt with the more familiar problem of alcoholism,[2]

---

1   Canon lawyers seem to agree on this: "Though cited at times as a problem, canon law was not really the problem. The problem was the bishops' reluctance to utilize the then-existing provisions of canon law for removing priests from ministry. The canonical tools were there" (Sister Sharon Euart, "Canon Law and Clergy Sexual Abuse Crisis: An Overview of the U.S. Experience," USCCB/CLSA Seminar presentation, May 25, 2010, http://www.usccb.org/issues-and -action/child-and-youth-protection/upload/USCCB-CANON-LAW-SEMINAR-2010 -EUART.pdf); "I do not see this [abuse crisis] as a failure of canon law," says Nicholas Cafardi, dean emeritus of the Duquesne University Law School and also a trained canon lawyer. "I think the deficiency was *the failure to use the system*. Most of the cases in the Pennsylvania grand jury report happened before 1990," Cafardi notes. "Even in those years it was a canonical crime for a clergyman to sexually abuse a child. They should have been processed under the canon law, and they weren't" (Tom Gjelten, "Has Catholic Canon Law Aggravated the Clergy Abuse Crisis?," National Public Radio, September 4, 2018, https://www.npr.org/2018/09/04/644667657 /has-catholic-canon-law-aggravated-the-clergy-abuse-crisis).

2   Cf. Philip Jenkins, *Pedophiles and Priests: Anatomy of a Contemporary Crisis* (Oxford: Oxford University Press, 1996), 91.

including using some of the same treatment facilities.[3] The alternative, extracanonical process that diocesan chanceries and their expert psychiatric consultants developed piecemeal over time basically involved the following process: sacramental Confession, treating the patient with a twelve-step program or other form of psychiatric therapy, assessing the risk of returning him to ministry, and keeping the incident quiet to avoid the dual sins of detraction against a priest's reputation (see *CCC* 2477–79) and of scandal to the faithful (*CCC* 2489–92). Let us consider how such a process can be defensible and even good in certain circumstances.

Confession. Some years ago, I heard the confession of an old man who had been a pedophile and for decades had sexually abused various children. He himself had been sexually abused as a child, and his own pedophilia was very much a response to the spiritual damage from that sin. He had been baptized, had fallen away from the Church for a long time, and yet toward the end of his life wanted to come back to the Church and be reconciled with God. And so, I heard his confession and gave him absolution. And, assuming he did his penance, his sins were forgiven. Despite his monstrous crimes, he was not a monster but a child of God, a prodigal son who had returned. There is, our Lord tells us, much rejoicing in Heaven over his confession and contrition (Lk 15:10). Any confessor should show sacramental mercy to such a penitent and should be happy afterward.

---

3   See Linda Matchan and Stephen Kurkjian, "Porter's Treatment Questioned," *Boston Globe*, July 16, 1992, http://archive.boston.com/globe/spotlight/abuse/archives/071692_porter.htm. "A top official in the St. Louis Diocese [*sic*] yesterday acknowledged that while he was the parish priest at St. Peter's Church in Kirkwood, Mo., that he would often use priests being treated at another halfway house operated by the Paraclete's treatment. Bishop Edward J. O'Donnell, vicar general in St. Louis, said he was surprised to learn that some of those residing at the halfway house, like Porter, were being treated for sexual abuse problems. 'My understanding is that they were all recovering alcoholics,' O'Donnell said. 'If I had known that, I might have taken a different attitude toward bringing them in.'"

Psychiatric therapy. In 1992, Michael Kelley, a convicted two-time rapist, was on parole from the Massachusetts
Treatment Center for the Sexually Dangerous when he lured
two women into his workplace and murdered them. A review
board had decided that Kelley was no longer sexually dangerous and granted him parole. In response to the spectacular
error in judgment, the administration of Republican Gover-
nor Bill Weld was contemplating closing down the treatment
facility (the only one in Massachusetts) and placing its inmate
patients in prisons. In response, the *Boston Globe* ran a front-
page story[4] and editorial[5] calling attention to the wonderful
work that psychiatrists were doing in curing sex offenders
and how a more carefully run program could be beneficial
for Massachusetts. A month later, in the midst of the scandal over Father James Porter's abuse of children in the Fall
River diocese, the *Globe* returned to this theme in an article
exploring the wonderful new treatments for priests who were
sex abusers, which in some cases allowed them to return to
ministry with "only" a 10 percent recidivism rate.[6] The point
of the article was to contrast this new treatment with the less
successful type of treatment that Porter had received. From
the perspective of behavior change therapy, a recidivism rate
of 10 percent is much better than the untreated rate of 40

---

4   Alison Bass, "New Therapy Seen to Cut Repeat Sex Crimes," *Boston Globe*, June 18, 1992,
http://www.themediareport.com/wp-content/uploads/2015/02/1992-Globe-New-therapy-seen
-to-cut-repeat-sex-crimes.pdf.
5   *Boston Globe* Editorial Board, "An Offender's Right to Treatment," *Boston Globe*, June 26,
1992, http://themediareport.com/wp-content/uploads/2015/02/1992-Globe-A-right-to-treatment
.pdf.
6   "Officials of three of the four leading centers that treat priest sex offenders—Southdown
near Toronto, St. Luke Institute in Maryland, and the Institute of Living in Hartford—said in
interviews last week that improved treatment yields great success, with as little as a 10 percent
recidivism rate. They and other specialists said many offenders can be returned to active ministry
so long as the clergy and their supervisors accept lifelong restrictions and follow-up care." James
L. Franklin, "Ways Cited to Treat Priests Who Abuse," *Boston Globe*, July 19, 1992, http://cache
.boston.com/globe/spotlight/abuse/archives/071992_porter.htm.

percent, and so both the *Globe* and the psychiatrists themselves could see their work as successful.

Protecting reputations. The decision not to publicize the sins of priests who were taken out of ministry and then returned to ministry was in accord with Catholic doctrine. The Code of Canon Law (can. 220) says, "No one is permitted to harm illegitimately the good reputation which a person possesses nor to injure the right of any person to protect his or her own privacy." The *Catechism* likewise declares, "Respect for the reputation of persons forbids every attitude and word likely to cause them unjust injury. He becomes guilty ... of detraction who, without objectively valid reason, discloses another's faults and failings to persons who did not know them" (2477). Someone who reveals something that damages another's reputation (even something true) offends against justice and charity (2479), unless there is a weighty and proportionate reason (2491). From this perspective, the Church officials were right not to publicize the sins of priests, whose reputation could be easily damaged by this sort of negative publicity. It was better to explain to people, "Father is not well," and then place him on medical leave where he could receive treatment. And if the psychiatrists pronounced him cured and fit for ministry, then secrecy was even more important to protect his ability to serve as a spiritual leader in the new assignment. So long as the psychiatrists were right and he was no longer a danger to anyone, for the Church officials to publicize his name risked serious sin.

As we all know to our immense sorrow and shame, the intersection of these well-meaning policies, each of them justified from a certain point of view, was a catastrophe that harmed hundreds and hundreds of people. What went wrong? First, the bishops and psychiatrists misjudged the risks that abuse and abusers present to the common good. Second, they misunderstood their spheres of responsibility.

What Went Wrong?

The bishops' decisions about whether to return an abusive priest to ministry relied on the judgments of psychiatrists, who (1) failed to understand how resistant to therapy sex abusers can be, and who (2) until the 1980s almost completely neglected the long-term consequences of abuse for the victims.[7] Partly this second mistake was a result of a selection bias: since the priests were being sent by the diocese to therapy, while the victims were not, the therapists understandably focused on the priests and their psychiatric care. As psychiatrists, their focus was on their patients, and for a time, only the priests were patients. But it also seems that psychiatry in the 1960s and 1970s was not sufficiently mature as a practice to offer competent consultation on criminal behavior. As we saw at the end of the last chapter, when prisons began to replace punishment with rehabilitative therapy, crime waves resulted. The same approach within the Church, replacing criminal proceedings with therapy, led to an analogous crime wave during more or less the same era.

Reformers in the Church who were in tune with the times embarked on a decades-long experiment, hoping that rehabilitative therapy could work for abusers as it had for alcoholics. They replaced punishment with leniency, turned leniency into a bureaucratic procedure, and did damage to the common good as a result (as our analysis suggested it would). The

---

7   Jenkins, *Pedophiles and Priests*, 140; see also 83–90. Also, Mark E. Chopko, "A Response to Timothy Lytton: More Conversation Is Needed," *Connecticut Law Review* 39, no. 3 (February 2007): 897–912.

problem is not with their goal of rehabilitation for the criminal, but with the risks they took in reintegrating the abuser into ministry. The risk to the common good that an alcoholic priest presents is different and usually much lower than the risk that an abuser presents, and so the threshold for reintegration should have been higher for abusers. The Church had for centuries distinguished these two cases, but many people in the Church, possessed by an optimistic belief in the power of therapy, set that wisdom aside.

The responsibility for the decision to trust the psychiatrists, ultimately, rests with the bishops. It seems as though part of the problem was that the bishops misunderstood the scope of their responsibility, and therefore the scope of their mercy. If the bishop were responsible only for the abusive priest, then mercy would demand that he be patient with him as with any sinner, granting forgiveness and helping him to begin his life again, perhaps in a different locale. But the bishop has direct responsibility for his entire diocese, especially the laity, and he has an indirect responsibility before God even for the non-Catholics in the boundaries of his diocese, and in a wider sense, he has the responsibility of reconciling all creation to its Creator.

These responsibilities are not on the same level—the bishop has to answer more directly for the souls of the Catholics in his diocese than for the souls of others—but they are real. And because they are real, and extensive, they put limits on how lenient and patient he can be with abusive clergy. From the perspective of the psychiatrist, if only 10 percent of abusive priests were to abuse in the future, his treatment program would be a success. But from the perspective of the bishop governing the diocese, a single case of recidivism would arguably be too much to risk—especially because abuse can have long-term effects upon the victim.

A bishop's sphere of responsibility changes his calculations of risk and legitimate self-defense from those of the psychiatrist or the confessor, and so his flexibility to show mercy was different as well. To whom more has been given, more will be demanded.

The Law-and-Order Backlash in the Church

In the 1980s, the law-and-order backlash against the crime waves of the previous decade renounced rehabilitation as a goal of criminal punishment and limited the discretion of judges to enact lenient sentences by passing sentencing guidelines such as "three strikes and you're out" laws. After the explosion of reports about abusive priests in the early 2000s, once again there was a law-and-order backlash, which also renounced rehabilitation and judicial discretion. The Dallas Charter for the Protection of Youth removed much of the flexibility that chancery officials had exercised before, in favor of a cut-and-dried procedure for dealing with priests accused of abuse. You could say that the zero-tolerance policy of the Dallas Charter serves as the Catholic version of sentencing guidelines.

I do not envy the bishops who have to handle these sorts of messes, and this chapter is not the place to analyze the Church's policies in response to the crisis. But I do want to call attention to a tendency in the Church to give in to virtue signaling and the mindset of the social media mobs, in which many Catholics rush to dehumanize the abusers.

Someone recently sent me a link to a homily by the rector of his diocese's cathedral in which he called a priest abuser "a fiend," a "carnivore" who had "amputated himself from the Church." The person who sent me the link called it "a homily we all need to hear." But imagine if the penitent pedophile whose confession I heard had been in that priest's congregation that day. Would he have gone to Confession if he heard that he was not part of the Church? If not, then the fiery homily might very well have *reduced* the rejoicing in Heaven. Catholics need to love their enemies and pray for the conversion of sinners. We must incapacitate them from doing further harm, and that often means incapacitating them for life. But we should never break solidarity with them.

Sean Cardinal O'Malley, one of the Church's most experienced leaders on this issue, uses language that delicately addresses this problem:

> Some of the most deeply moving moments that I have experienced in the course of meetings with survivors and family members have been when men and women who have suffered the most egregious abuse, even the death of a loved one, tell me that they are striving each day to forgive the man who abused them and in fact pray for him as part of their daily prayers. This is an extraordinary and humbling sign of God's goodness beyond all measure. May we join the example of our brothers and sisters in Christ praying for those men who have committed most grievous sins and crimes against children. May they receive the grace to turn to the mercy of God seeking the gift of repentance and atonement.[8]

This sort of pastoral encouragement for forgiveness ought to be a model for others. The Church ought to do less virtue signaling and scapegoating, and more to encourage reconciliation, mercy, solidarity, and forgiveness, as a way of growing stronger.

---

8   Sean Cardinal O'Malley, "Open Letter to Survivors," website of the Archdiocese of Boston, accessed November 14, 2020, https://www.bostoncatholic.org/protecting-children-word-welcome/open-letter-survivors.

The Church's Teaching on Capital Punishment

In the fall of 2018, Pope Francis ordered that the *Catechism of the Catholic Church* be changed, with the goal of encouraging all Catholics to advocate for the abolition of the death penalty. The decision to publish this in the *Catechism*, and arguments made in the changed text, were confusing to many people, which makes me think that there might have been a better way for the pope to explain his decision. But while the reasons for the teaching are not evident to everyone, the pope's marching orders are clear: "The Church ... works with determination for [the death penalty's] abolition worldwide" (*CCC* 2267).

When Pope Saint John Paul II addressed capital punishment in his Encyclical Letter on the Gospel of Life, *Evangelium Vitae* (March 25, 1995), he taught that the only grounds for executing a prisoner were those of legitimate self-defense.

> The nature and extent of the punishment must be carefully evaluated and decided upon, and ought not go to the extreme of executing the offender except in cases of absolute necessity: in other words, when it would not be possible otherwise to defend society. Today however, as a result of steady improvements in the organization of the penal system, such cases are very rare, if not practically non-existent. (56)

We can understand the sort of calculation encouraged here: if the criminal is incapacitated so that he presents no threat to society, then there is no need to incapacitate him further by killing him. If he still presents a threat, and it is not possible to incapacitate him enough that others (including other prisoners) are safe, then it might be necessary to kill him out of self-defense. In advanced countries with supermax prison technology, that would rarely become necessary. Mercy requires us to do our best to treat even our most threatening prisoners with solidarity, so long as society is protected.

The evolution of the Church's teaching on the death penalty comes out of a larger movement since Vatican II to think more theologically about questions of politics and society. Whenever the Church reflects upon God's treatment of sinners, it emphasizes that God's punishments are medicinal and disciplinary, that God wants the conversion of sinners and not their death, that that he punishes reluctantly not vindictively. Both God and Satan agree on our sins, but Satan condemns us out of malice, while God sends his Son to save us. The Church's own internal treatment of sinners is modeled after the method of fraternal correction explained by Jesus and practiced by the apostles. It should not surprise us if, after the Church reflects more on how and why God punishes us, and how and why we respond to sinners the way we do, that it should extend these same principles to how political society ought to think about violations of justice.

9

The Merciful Discipline of God the Father

We began this book with a theological puzzle about God's mercy: How could the God who insists that he is merciful at the same moment command the harshest of punishments? Why does God throughout the Bible associate mercy with crushing his enemies? Why does God order the Israelites to show no mercy to their pagan enemies and say that this command originates in his mercy and love? The Church's tradition has ruled heretical the interpretive approach of Marcionism, which claims that the Old Testament got a wrong picture of God as wrathful, which the New Testament picture of God as merciful has superseded. It is also heretical to think that Jesus' merciful will is opposed to the Father's wrathful will. As we have repeatedly emphasized, Jesus commands us to be merciful as our Heavenly Father is merciful, and in the Garden of Gethsemane he unites his will to the Father's. Jesus is very clear that at the end of time there will be some who are cast out into eternal punishment and condemnation, a fate more severe than even the ban. All the favorite solutions to the puzzle (ignore the Old Testament, ignore the Father's mercy, ignore Jesus' willingness to condemn and punish, adopt the Marcionite or universalist heresies) are not available to an orthodox Christian who reads Scripture closely.

We have spent much of the first part of the book thinking about mercy as a political idea: the limitations of justice-only politics, the problems of thinking about mercy as lenience or tolerance, and how mercy contributes to solidarity and stability within society. We explored some of the conceptual and philosophical problems that come from punishing without mercy and have sketched some principles of punishing that try to correct and reintegrate the offender while protecting society at the same time. It was necessary to rethink punishment and justice and mercy as we have done, because only by reforming our understanding of those concepts can we solve the puzzle we faced at the beginning. In this chapter, we will see that "restorative solidarity" characterizes God's mercy, and pedagogical punishment is the consistent model of punishment that God uses after the Fall, from the Old Testament throughout the New, from Genesis to Revelation.

The Second Vatican Council's Dogmatic Constitution on Divine Revelation, *Dei Verbum* (November 18, 1965), insisted that the correct way to read the Old Testament is to see at work a "divine pedagogy" (15), in which God is training Israel and preparing a select group within Israel so that in "the fullness of time" (Gal 4:4) they would be able to receive Jesus and follow him. And part of that work involved protecting Israel from those who would destroy it or corrupt their relationship with God, whether through defeat in battle or through seducing God's people away from right worship. As the faith of Israel grew stronger, it was better prepared to deal with pagans without losing its way. When Jesus finally came, he could extend to the pagans God's covenant with Abraham, which Mary accurately describes in the Magnificat (see Lk 1:46–55) as God's promise of mercy.

In previous chapters we developed a view of mercy as a type of solidarity that restores justice. God certainly has this sort of solidarity with sinners: he wants them to change, and he is on their side. When he treats sinners harshly, it is both for their own good and for the common good. He combines the legitimate defense of the common good with a merciful desire to prepare his people for the coming of his Son. We have seen how this model of punishment can work in human contexts. In this chapter we will see how it can also explain many puzzling things about God's plan of salvation.

Incapacitation and Divine Punishment

Legitimate self-defense gives the punisher a reason to use coercive force to incapacitate an aggressor. And as we have seen, incapacitation is not the same as vengeance or retribution; one can incapacitate lovingly, as when a mother separates her quarrelling children, or when one takes away the driver's license of an aging parent. Many of God's most serious punishments can be sufficiently explained by his need to defend various goods from human wickedness and sin. Even the most terrifying punishments—including the ban in the Old Testament and condemnation to Hell in the New—are not in any way incompatible with his being merciful and in solidarity with those he incapacitates. Let us consider several of these biblical punishments.

The expulsion from Eden and the curse of death. After the Fall, Adam and Eve are banished from Eden to prevent them from eating from the fruit of the tree of life as they had eaten from the tree of knowledge (Gen 3:22–24). Imagine if God had not taken that precaution. Adam, Eve, and perhaps their descendants would have lived immortally in a fallen world with fallen souls, alienated from God, living selfish lives that could never end. This would be akin to Hell on earth, as the *Catechism* explains: "The chief punishment of hell is eternal separation from God, in whom alone man can possess the life and happiness for which he was created and for which he longs" (1035). From this perspective, we can see that introducing death into the human condition was medicinal, giving us a way to escape this vale of tears. And of course, if death were not possible, then Jesus could never have sacrificed himself on the Cross. Since Adam and Eve had shown that they could not be trusted to obey God's commands, he expelled them from Eden to separate them from the tree of immortal life, a form of incapacitation.

The Flood. Even after God cursed them with eventual death, the first men lived very long lives. Soon, God decided that a long life as a fallen human being was a bad thing, and that the people had too much time to do evil. To restrict their opportunity for wickedness, he limited all subsequent lives to 120 years (Gen 6:3), a limited form of incapacitation. But this limitation was not enough, as man's wickedness was the only thing to multiply and fill the earth (a corruption of the commandment to man before the Fall), and "every desire that their heart conceived was always nothing but evil" (Gen 6:5). God determined to uncreate the fallen and corrupted world (Gen 6:7–12) so as to restart a covenant with the righteous Noah (Gen 6:18). As we have seen, capital punishment is an extreme form of incapacitation. This terrible destruction did not get rid of the evil of the human heart (Gen 8:21), but it did reduce its effects, as all the long-lived and thoroughly wicked people were replaced by shorter-lived people descended from Noah's more pious family.

The Tower of Babel. As an incapacitating punishment, the confusion of languages is comparatively mild. But once again it puts a limit on human pride and ambition. The engineering achievement represented by the Tower showed that fallen man could use technology to increase the potency of its fallenness (Gen 11:6). Limiting fallen man's ability to work together thus limits the damage that technology can do in the wrong hands. God temporarily lifted the curse of Babel at Pentecost, showing how a Church of one heart and one mind united around prayer through the grace of the Spirit (Acts 4:32) does not pose any similar threat.

The ban. The word translated as "ban" in the Old Testament seems to have a dual meaning of being consecrated to God and being destroyed, a double meaning also reflected in the word "sacrifice" (literally "to make sacred," sometimes by killing and offering to God). It is first used in Numbers 21:1–3, when Israel offered to put the towns of Arad under the ban, and the Lord accepted the proposal, although something like it is proposed in Exodus 34:10–17 without using the word. It is not always clearly associated with killing the enemy, but it always does involve destroying the idols and religious places of the pagans and instituting some sort of complete separation from the conquered pagans, rather than the commonly accepted practices of enslaving conquered enemies and intermarrying with them. And, famously, it sometimes does involve the killing of captives (Num 31:14–18; 1 Sam 15:1–23; perhaps Deut 25:18–19), although some commentators note that it is always the prophet (e.g., Moses and Samuel) who commands the killing and wonder whether those were human additions to the divine will.

Regardless, the clearly stated goal of the ban is incapacitation, the defense of Israel's fragile existence and fragile faith from external threats and from seductive temptations. Whenever Israel does not keep the ban, they end up sinning, as God warned that they would. For example, the prediction that intermarriage with pagan captives will lead Israel to idolatry (Ex 34:17) is quickly proven right when they intermarry with the Moabite women and immediately begin to worship their god Baal (Num 25:1–2). Phineas, the priest and grandson of Aaron, makes himself forever a model of good Jewish zeal for the Lord when he drives a spear through one such coupling (Num 25:7–16), thus sparing Israel from God's punishment. To prevent Israel from falling to the daughters of Moab again,

Moses orders that all sexually experienced Moabite women be killed (Num 31:15–18). Later, when King Saul disobeys the ban, it is because he and his troops were tempted by greed for booty (1 Sam 15:9, 19).

The ban is actually more lenient as an incapacitating punishment than the Flood, since its goal is not an end to the wickedness of the pagans, but rather the preservation of Israel to serve as a leaven in the world. If God is right that it is not just the weapons but also the souls of the pagans that place Israel's future at risk, then God's actions would be legitimately acting in defense of the common good, which requires that Israel grow in love and obedience to God.

Hell and Purgatory. Hell is clearly another form of incapacitating punishment. Satan's being cast out of Heaven is similar to the exile of Adam and Eve from Eden but has a different purpose: the protection of Heaven as a perfect place, where God's will is perfectly done (Ps 24:4). Imagine if Hitler and Stalin and Mao and Pol Pot (and Satan) were able to still be mega-sinners while in Heaven—it would turn Heaven into another fallen place like earth. For Heaven to be a perfect place where God's will is done, God has to exclude from Heaven those who refuse to do his will.

Divine Punishment Teaches a Lesson

God's punishments are not simply to incapacitate those who threaten his plan for salvation, but also to teach and form Israel to do his will, as Moses explains in Deuteronomy 4:15–31. Moses is addressing the assembled nation of Israel before they cross the Jordan and enter the Promised Land. It is a dramatic renewal of the covenant that took place in Exodus, when God appeared to Israel, not in any visible form but only as a voice from within shapeless elements such as fire and clouds.

Moses reminds the people of this fact, that God does not have a shape and so cannot be represented by idols. If in the future, however, they were to repeat the sin of the golden calf and worship any sort of idol, they would be punished by losing the bounty that God has given them, and so be conquered:

> When you have children and children's children, and have grown old in the land, should you then act corruptly by fashioning an idol in the form of anything, and by this evil done in his sight provoke the LORD, your God, I call heaven and earth this day to witness against you, that you shall all quickly perish from the land which you are crossing the Jordan to possess. You shall not live in it for any length of time but shall be utterly wiped out. The LORD will scatter you among the peoples, and there shall remain but a handful of you among the nations to which the LORD will drive you. There you shall serve gods that are works of human hands, of wood and stone, gods which can neither see nor hear, neither eat nor smell. (Deut 4:25–28)

This is, of course, just what happened, first to Samaria and then later to Judah. Israel's infidelity led to their defeat and capture by pagans, who encouraged them to idolatry. But God's punishment of Israel is revealed here to be medicinal, not final, and the covenant will not be broken even though Israel has not kept up its end. Instead, the punishment will make them realize the extent of their folly, and the powerlessness of the pagan "gods":

> Yet when you seek the LORD, your God, from [those foreign places], you shall indeed find him if you search after him with all your heart and soul. In your distress, when all these things shall have come upon you, you shall finally return to the LORD, your God, and listen to his voice. Since the LORD, your

> God, is a merciful God, he will not abandon or destroy you,
> nor forget the covenant with your ancestors that he swore to
> them. (Deut 4:29–31)

God promises Israel that if they sin, he will teach them a lesson—a painful lesson, but one that he explains by appealing to
his mercy. Earlier, we saw that pedagogical punishment must
always take place within a context of solidarity. God's pedagogical punishment always takes place in the context of his
covenant with Israel, which God refuses to break even though
he has reason to. And this covenantal solidarity is identified
with God's mercy.

Divine Forgiveness and Rehabilitation

When developing our theory of punishment, we also saw that
the period of incapacitation should end when the offender
does not present a danger to the common good of society.
God does the same thing in the passage we are examining,
when he agrees to cease punishing Israel once they renounce
their idolatry and search for God "with all [their] heart and
soul." Israel's wholehearted repentance brings with it God's
wholehearted forgiveness. Why? Because God, who knows
the hearts of us all, knows that when the repentance is wholehearted, the offender does not present a danger to the common good.

  Let us define some terms. Repentance is when an offender,
while acknowledging that his past actions were wrong, from
now on decides to be a different kind of person, one who
will not do that sin again. An apology is the expression of
repentance to the injured party or parties. Forgiveness is when
the injured party decides to separate in some sense the past
wrongful act from the person who committed it. Forgiveness

can be partial (I forgive you, but I cannot trust you), or it can be complete (it is as if the sin never happened). In ordinary contexts of punishment, it can be hard to know whether someone has repented wholeheartedly. We might demand an apology, which is some evidence that a person repents, but that might not be sufficient evidence for us, especially if complete forgiveness involves a great risk. In God's case, because God knows our wills, there is no risk, and he can cease to punish immediately after the repentance.

God's demand of Israel, then, is that the repentance be wholehearted: "You shall indeed find him if you search after him with all your heart and soul." The language here prefigures the famous commandment of a few chapters later: "You shall love the Lord, your God, with your whole heart, and with your whole being, and with your whole strength" (Deut 6:5). If the Israelites love God with their whole being, if their contrition is complete, God is satisfied and will stop punishing them. Paradoxically, God's goal in punishing Israel is to elicit Israel's love. Like an alcoholic hitting rock bottom, the Israelites must recognize that they need a higher power to save them. Even the punishment of being banished from the Promised Land and stripped of all God's gifts is meant to teach Israel that it is God, not themselves or Baal, who gave them the gifts in the first place (cf. Hos 2:7–10).

From Israel's perspective, God's mercy and fidelity are two of the most surprising and wonderful features about their relationship with God. God will punish them, but he will never abandon them. As we saw earlier, God defines himself in one of the most solemn moments of the Old Testament as "gracious and merciful, slow to anger and abounding in love and fidelity, continuing his love for a thousand generations, and for-giving wickedness, rebellion, and sin" (Ex 34:6–7). This description of God is so important that the Bible repeats it again and again, especially when Israel has sinned and looks for God's mercy (see Num 14:18; Jer 32:18; Lam 2:13; Bar 2:11—3:8; Jon 4:2). The Israelites in the period of the judges would sin, be faced with a mortal peril by an external enemy, and then appeal to God's mercy to save them, knowing that God was punishing them for their infidelity but also that in his mercy he would never break covenant with them (see Judg 3:7–9ff.; Ps 86:14–15). The wise King Solomon, in his long prayer dedicating the Temple, anticipates that Israel will sin and forget their side of the covenant, so Solomon repeatedly petitions God to show mercy and forgiveness whenever they cry out to him (1 Kings 8:22–53). Over and over, God's punishment is seen as a way to bring the Israelites back to right worship, to teach them a lesson, to discipline them. God does not punish out of malice, but out of love of Israel.

Fear of the Lord as a Deterrent to Sin

Awareness that God punishes and disciplines and incapacitates also can instill in us what the Bible calls "fear of the Lord."

> This is why you put into our hearts the fear of you: that we may call upon your name, and praise you in our exile, when we have removed from our hearts all the wickedness of our ancestors who sinned against you. (Bar 3:7)

Many Christians, and even many rabbis, have tried to make this sort of fear into something other than fear, but that is a mistake. Fear of the Lord is an awareness that God does in fact punish sinners, a warning not to take his mercy and patience for granted, a grace that fights against the sin of presumption. Fear of the Lord plays a significant part in Old Testament spirituality (see Deut 10:12; Ps 33:8; 34:9; Prov 1:7; 8:13; 14:26–27), and it is in no way absent from the New Testament (see Mt 10:28; Lk 1:50; Phil 2:12–13). As we mentioned earlier, it is one of the seven gifts of the Holy Spirit (Is 11:2–3), which Jesus himself possesses (Lk 4:18–21); as such, this fear must be totally consistent with the New Testament emphasis on mercy and love.

The devil tries to corrupt this fear into a type of terror at God, which is especially characteristic of those who have the spiritual disease of scruples, in which a person thinks God is looking for the merest excuse to condemn him. That type of fear the tradition calls "servile fear," and it is a spiritual error that involves a false picture of God (Lk 11:13). True fear of the Lord, rather, "is the beginning of wisdom" (Ps 111:10). It is a great spiritual help (a grace of the Spirit), at least in the sense that, if you have a healthy respect for God's willingness to punish disobedience, it helps your cost-benefit analysis to be more accurate. You start to think, "Hmm, let us see ... if I obey God, I'll receive eternal happiness in the life to come, but there is this temptation to sin over there which promises immediate happiness; oh wait, if I sin, I'll be punished worse than that little bit of happiness; therefore, I'll try to avoid sin." Fear of the Lord regarding Original Sin makes us aware that, on our own merits, we do not deserve to be in Heaven, and must cling closely to God's saving power.

In one of the formulas for the Act of Contrition in Confession, people say, "O my God, I am heartily sorry for having offended thee, and I detest all my sins, because I dread the loss of Heaven, and the pains of Hell; but most of all because they offend thee, my God, who are all good and deserving of all my love." Dreading the loss of Heaven and the pains of Hell are lesser but still legitimate reasons for not wanting to sin. The better reason is *because* "God is deserving of all my love," we should love God with all our heart. But as a backup, our self-interest in not going to Hell can help give us an extra motivational boost.

God Taught, Israel Eventually Learned

We can understand God's punishing if we remember that mercy is not about leniency but about promoting a greater justice. God's goal for mankind is always that more and more people be lifted up out of sin so that their broken hearts can be fully restored and thus they will be able to enjoy friendship with him. His saving action requires our willing cooperation. His plan for salvation required that the Jews be prepared to accept Jesus eventually, and so serious-enough threats to the Jewish nation or Israel's faith required serious reactions. Our sense of morality assumes that God's commands here cannot be justified, let alone be attributed to mercy, since we would be wrong if we were to slaughter noncombatants in war. But we should remember that we are at a different stage in salvation history than Moses' people, that our temptation to idolatry is lesser, and, thanks to the grace won for us by Christ, our faith is stronger.

As we saw in earlier chapters, mercy requires strength. As Israel grew in strength of faith, it was in less danger from paganism. We know that the complete separation from the pagans, which God commands here, was already mitigated later in the Old Testament—the book of Ruth, for instance, celebrates a Jewish-pagan intermarriage. God's punishment of exiling the Jews from their land, to everyone's surprise, made them stronger and purer in their faith. The end of the Babylonian Captivity saw a faithful remnant of the Jews return to Israel after having passed through a crucible in which their faith survived despite decades of totalitarian attempts to root it out. In fact, the Old Testament story after the return from

Babylon is largely a story of Jewish zeal. They learned their lesson and were stronger for it. God's harsh punishment for their infidelity was strong medicine that left them firmly committed to follow his law. They became law-abiding citizens, the goal of all merciful, pedagogical punishment. And they were prepared, in the fullness of time, to receive God's Son.

10

Original Justice, Original Sin, Jesus' Covenant

When the apostles ask Jesus how to pray, he tells them to pray, "Your will be done, on earth as in heaven" (Mt 6:10). Our Lord, in his great priestly prayer at the Last Supper, prayed that all his followers may be united to one another and to God in Heaven (Jn 17:20–26), a prayer that was answered in the early Church, which, filled by the Holy Spirit after Pentecost, was "of one heart and mind" (Acts 4:32). Saint Paul tells the Corinthians, "Whoever is joined to the Lord becomes one spirit with him" (1 Cor 6:17). For this reason, the spiritual tradition of the Church describes the heights of holiness as the "unitive way" and "the imitation of Christ." Justice is when things are rightly ordered. Since God is justice itself, God's will is perfectly just. In the case of human beings, justice is when we participate in God's justice, when our wills are ordered by God's will, when we want what he wants because he wants it. When Saint Paul talks about "justification," this is the goal: that our wills be made right and just the way God intended for them to be, choosing the right thing for the right reason.

In Heaven, God's Will Is Done Perfectly

Heaven is supposed to be a place where everyone is a saint; where everyone loves God with all his heart, strength, soul, and mind; where everyone loves God more than anything else; and where everyone obeys God in every detail simply out of his tremendous love of God. Scripture insists that we need to be perfect to be in Heaven. "Who may go up the mountain of the LORD?" asks the Psalmist. "The clean of hand and pure of heart, who has not given his soul to useless things" (Ps 24:3–4). If any animal sacrificed to God must be unblemished, because nothing corrupt can be in the presence of the holy on earth, how much more is Heaven to be preserved from corruption?

God cannot allow Heaven to be fallen the way that earth is fallen. If that were to happen, then there would be no place of justice anywhere in creation, no place where God was effective as a ruler. That is equivalent to saying that God would be a failure as king; and it is blasphemous to argue that God is a failure. He must exclude from Heaven anyone whose will is not in accord with his, who acts from a motive other than justice, other than because he said so. His will must be done in Heaven, and only those whose will is united to his can be in Heaven.

Earlier we referenced the classic debate about whether a society would be more stable if governed by love of justice or fear of punishment. We argued that love creates a more stable society, as all those in it act positively to support society's good, rather than look solely to their own interests. Heaven is a perfectly stable society in this sense, a society in which everyone loves the same things and is motivated by his love.

In the early moments of creation, some angels rebelled and were punished; after seeing the terrible incapacitating punishment of Hell, nobody who resisted the temptation to disobey God that first time could ever find disobedience tempting ever again. The deterrence effect of Hell, the fear of the Lord, protects the saints from ever wandering away from the love of God's will. Every citizen in Heaven is forever a law-abiding citizen.

Original Sin and Its Effect

In the beginning, God created Adam and Eve with the gift of original justice and charity—the ability to love God in himself simply because he is the being most worth loving that could possibly exist. Before the Fall, Adam and Eve could act without making any reference to themselves, simply out of the love of God. They could serve God easily and happily, without asking, "What's in it for me?" and without worrying whether they would receive a reward for their service or be punished were they not to serve. They were law-abiding citizens of God's Kingdom, for a time.

After the Fall, they and their descendants lost this ability to love God with all their hearts, with charity. We could still love God after some fashion, but we could only love him with reference to ourselves. We could love God for what he does for us—if he does good things for us, if he answers our prayers. And we could obey God out of fear of going to Hell, which would be bad for us. But in these cases, we really would not love God so much as we loved ourselves. We treat God as a means to our own ends, to our self-love. More and less subtle forms of pride and self-love predominate, as Saint Paul describes to Timothy: "People will be self-centered and lovers of money, proud, haughty, abusive, disobedient to their parents, ungrateful, irreligious, callous, implacable, slanderous, licentious, brutal, hating what is good, traitors, reckless, conceited, lovers of pleasure rather than lovers of God" (2 Tim 3:2–4). Saint Augustine wrote that the city of God was made up of those who loved God to the exclusion of the love of themselves. After the Fall, no human being was capable of loving God in this sort of way. That is the essential effect of Original Sin. And it follows from this that no human being belongs in the city of God, that in justice no human person belongs in Heaven, because our wills are not united to God's.

Framing the problem this way reveals some of God's difficulty in saving us. Original Sin is not something merely attributed to us from the outside; it is something fundamentally broken about us on the inside. Original Sin is a privation, in which we are missing something that we ought to have—namely, charity, the ability to love God and obey him simply because it is right and just to do so. Which means that to forgive our sins requires more than simply deciding not to apply an extrinsic penalty; it requires fixing something deep within us.

Original Sin has left our hearts diseased, not fit enough for the rigors of heavenly love. We lost half of the proper functioning of our hearts; we lost our former ability to love God simply for his own sake. God cannot pretend we do not have Original Sin any more than a cardiologist can pretend a patient does not have heart disease. Ignoring the problem does not make it better. Heart disease cannot just be left alone to run its course; it requires action on the part of the doctor. So too with God. Our hearts will not get better unless (to borrow a famous image from the prophet Ezekiel) we can get a heart transplant: "I will give you a new heart, and a new spirit I will put within you. I will remove the heart of stone from your flesh and give you a heart of flesh" (Ezek 36:26). We need a new heart—Jesus' Sacred Heart—if we are to love as we ought (Jn 15:12), if we are to be able to love God to the point of sacrificing ourselves and our self-interest.

Happiness in Heaven

It is not that God is mad at us and could forgive us once he gets over his anger. It is that after Original Sin, human beings are unable to be happy even in Heaven. Why? Because we are not able to do what Heaven requires. Even if fallen human beings were admitted to Heaven, we would be miserable, like the way the prophet Isaiah was miserable during his vision of Heaven. Isaiah was watching the seraphim worship God and hearing their song of praise rock the very lintels of the heavenly Temple (Is 6:2–4). And what was his first reaction? "Woe is me" (Is 6:5). Not, "Let me sing along with the heavenly chorus," but despair: "I am doomed." Isaiah knew that he could not sing the song of the angels, "Holy, holy, holy, Lord God of Hosts," with his unclean lips.

That is the problem that faces every person born under Original Sin: even if we were to see Heaven, we would not enjoy it, because we would know we were not worthy. In the image Jesus uses in the parable of the wedding feast (Mt 22:11), we would be underdressed. Unless we can be made better than we are, unless we were once again able to love God with all our hearts, even being in Heaven would be a kind of misery for us. God could not bring a sinner into Heaven without doing something unjust to that person. None of us belong in Heaven thanks to the corruption of Original Sin, in the same way that no corrupted and blemished animal was appropriate for sacrifices in the Temple, and nobody unworthy could enter the presence of God in the Temple.

To summarize God's problem in saving us: God's justice requires him (1) to keep Heaven perfect and (2) to admit some imperfect human beings into Heaven. Of course, he must also (3) respect their freedom of will (for example, he cannot simply turn us into obedient zombies). And (4) he cannot manipulate human beings or bribe them into loving him by appealing to their self-interest, since that would be to obey God for the wrong reasons, for reasons of self-love and not of justice itself. A further problem is that we human beings lack the power to fix each other. (Remember that the person who helps another cannot be suffering from the same privation or deficiency; and after Original Sin all human beings suffer from the same unjust wills.) Therefore, God's justice requires (5) that God must save human beings himself.

How Jesus' Sacrifice Earns Our Consecration

Pope Benedict XVI teaches that

> being saved does not mean merely escaping punishment but being delivered from the evil that dwells within us. It is not punishment that must be eliminated but sin, the rejection of God and of love. (General Audience, May 18, 2011)

God so loved the world that in the fullness of time he sent his only Son to become incarnate and offer himself as the unblemished sacrifice for our sins. That is the Good News, the story of our salvation. As a sinless man, Jesus was not subject to the curse of Adam that he must die (see Gen 3:19; Rom 5:12–14). Rather than insist on his right as a sinless man not to die, Jesus generously offered his life as a sacrifice to the Father. As God, Jesus was equal to the Father in all things. As man, he owed God the Father perfect obedience of the will (Heb 10:7). But because he was sinless, he did not owe God his death (Jn 10:18). When he offered his life, then, it was as a sacrifice, something he consecrated to God as a free gift (Jn 17:19).

Jesus' gift was not primarily the flesh of the sacrifice. Indeed, even the Old Testament points out several times that the value of a sacrifice is in the love and the will of the person sacrificing (see 1 Sam 15:22; Is 1:10–20; Hos 6:6; Amos 5:22–25; Mic 6:6–8; Ps 40:7–9). As Pope Saint John Paul II writes in his Encyclical Letter on the Eucharist in Its Relationship to the Church, *Ecclesia de Eucharistia* (April 17, 2003), "Jesus' gift of his love and obedience to the point of giving his life is in the first place a gift to his Father. Certainly, it is a gift given for our sake, and indeed that of all humanity … yet it is *first and foremost a gift to the Father*: 'a sacrifice that the Father accepted' (Phil. 2:8)" (13; italics in original). Jesus' sacrificial gift of himself showed God his generosity and love.

There is a sense in which Jesus' gift puts God the Father into his debt. Jesus had not only kept all God's commandments, but he had done more than he needed to do. Therefore, it would have been wrong if God had not given Jesus back something in return. Sacrifices seal covenants with God the way giving gifts seals covenants between equals. As both God and man, Jesus' sacrifice was at the same time a gift between equals and the seal of a New Covenant. Jesus' priestly prayer at the Last Supper is not merely asking the Father nicely for favors; rather, he is negotiating a covenant: "I glorified you on earth by accomplishing the work that you gave me to do. Now glorify me, Father, with you, with the glory that I had with you before the world began" (Jn 17:4–5).

But this creates a problem in Trinitarian theology: How can God the Father repay God the Son? What can he give him that he does not already have? The only thing that differentiates the Father from the Son is the Father's paternity, his being the Father, which, of course, he cannot give away. He has nothing to give to Jesus in his divinity; he can only give gifts to Jesus in his created humanity.

First, he can give Jesus the power of resurrection and ascension into Heaven in body as well as soul (Jn 17:5), a power beyond Jesus' human nature. Second, he can give Jesus the power to unite other human beings to his resurrected Mystical Body, consecrating them and joining them to his sacrifice (Jn 17:17–19; Heb 10:10), by which the Father will adopt them as his own children. In his priestly prayer at the Last Supper, Jesus says of the apostles and all who believe because of them that they are God's "gift" to him (Jn 17:24), a gift in response to Jesus' sacrificial gift, a Church to whom Jesus communicates his grace, his holiness, his truth, his glory, his joy, and his unity with the Father in charity.

The Father's covenant with Jesus includes the gift of salvation for all those who have faith in his Son. As a result of this New Covenant, Jesus offers to his followers the chance to heal their hearts. His sacrifice merited him the ability to give eternal life and his glory (Jn 17:2, 22), a share in the rewards for his sacrifice, to all who believe in him. Because this is part of the covenant, in exchange for Jesus' sacrifice, this offer of merciful healing is a part of divine justice.

But Jesus is still constrained by the same problem as before: human free will. How could a people who since the Fall had been living only for their own self-interest, and who had developed sophisticated and subtle forms of self-love as defense mechanisms in a fallen world, begin to love God selflessly, with all their hearts? The Polish mystic Saint Faustina gave the answer when she placed the words "Jesus, I trust in you" on her famous image of Divine Mercy, insightfully tying together the theme of mercy and the theme of trust. Jesus can give all the gifts he won from the Father to those who trust in him. When Jesus says, "I pray not only for them [the apostles], but also for those who will believe in me through their word" (Jn 17:20), the word "believe" in Greek does not mean a merely intellectual assent, but also fidelity and trust. To believe, to have faith, is to entrust one's heart and mind and will to Jesus, to subordinate ourselves to him completely.

Trust in Jesus Is the Only Path to Salvation

To trust in Jesus means that we stop trusting in our own judgment, that we stop analyzing our rational self-interest, balancing costs and benefits: "Everyone of you who does not renounce all his possessions cannot be my disciple" (Lk 14:33). Trusting in Jesus means that we follow him even when we do not like where he seems to be going (see Jn 11:16; 21:18–19). To follow him wherever he may go, even to the Cross, even to suffering and death—to trust him even when our self-protective instincts are screaming at us that this will be painful—is the only path to salvation. The idea is not merely that we love something more than ourselves, that any sort of sacrifice is equally effective at overcoming our selfishness. We must trust in the Person of Jesus, and only in him. Throughout the Gospels, nothing is more infuriating to Jesus than when people do not trust him. This is not because he is egotistical, but because not trusting him cuts us off from the covenant and its mercy. At the beginning of the chapter, we said that God's goal for us is that our will be united with his. That is what it means for us to be holy, for our souls to be ordered as God wants. Since Jesus' will is identified with the Father's will, to unify our will with Jesus' is to be holy. If we do not follow him, our wills are not aligned with his, and we remain in our sin, separated from his gift of eternal life.

In the last chapter, we saw how God prepared Israel to learn to trust him. It involved many hard lessons, but over and over God would find a remnant of his people who followed even the most counterintuitive and difficult commandments faithfully. Throughout the Old Testament, God was preparing the people of Israel so that in the fullness of time there would be a portion of the people who could trust his Son when he came, despite all the reasons not to.

In the spiritual life of each Christian, this divine pedagogy is repeated. Even when we have been baptized and reborn in Christ as infants, growing up in this fallen world can still leave us scarred. Starting as children, in response to the spiritual disorder of our surroundings, we develop self-defense mechanisms. These work to protect us in this vale of tears, and they might even help us flourish for a time, but as they seduce us into trusting ourselves more and more, the hodgepodge of coping mechanisms that make up our personalities ultimately becomes an obstacle in our spiritual life.

Our very feelings can be an obstacle to faith. The Carmelite Doctors of the Church Saint Teresa of Avila and Saint John of the Cross describe in detail how all souls, even those who have grown closest to God, must go through a purification of their desires for comfort and even for spiritual consolations so that their self-love can be subdued and their charity, their love of God for his own sake, can flourish. Christian mortification and asceticism have the goal of training our bodies to submit to our souls and our souls to submit to the Holy Spirit.

Our self-image can also be an obstacle to faith. We can think of ourselves as smart or attractive or self-confident or athletic or middle-class or pious. All those things, no matter how true about us, are not descriptions of our true identity. We need to realize that *our relationship as sons and daughters of God* is the most important thing about us, that our Baptism ought to be the real basis of our self-image.

God teaches us and corrects us and disciplines us. He prunes us (Jn 15:2), as he pruned the Israelites, so that we can learn to rely on ourselves less and on him more and more. He prunes us through words (Jn 15:3), through suffering (Jas 1:2–4), and through our life experience. For those with eyes to see, God shows us the limits of our talents, he reveals his power, he proves his solidarity, he exposes the poverty of our love, and he teaches us humility. This is often painful, but it is tough love—the merciful action of a loving father (Heb 12:5–11).

11

Mercy and the Sacraments of Incorporation

All the faithful of the Church are part of Christ's Mystical Body (*CCC* 790), a truth which our Lord revealed to Saint Paul on the road to Damascus when he told him that to persecute Christians was to persecute him (Acts 9:4–5). This mysterious identity explains how the covenant with Jesus gets extended to some, but not all, of those who share his humanity. God's covenant is with Jesus, but since Jesus identifies himself with the Church (cf. Acts 22:8), God's covenant is also with the Church.

Twice in the Old Testament, with both Noah and Moses, God threatens to destroy everyone and make a new people out of one righteous man. With Noah, he basically went through with it. The problem is that because of Original Sin, even something that drastic will not work to fix us: "Since the desires of the human heart are evil from youth" (Gen 8:21). After Jesus' sacrifice on the Cross, his great gift that earned a great gift in return, God the Father finally gets to renew the human race—through Jesus. God's covenant is with Jesus; all those who *become Jesus* get to participate in the New Covenant.

Baptism Resurrects Us as Christ

According to the Code of Canon Law,

> Baptism, the gateway to the sacraments and necessary for salvation by actual reception or at least by desire, is validly conferred only by a washing of true water with the proper form of words. Through baptism men and women are freed from sin, are reborn as children of God, and, configured to Christ by an indelible character, are incorporated into the Church. (can. 849)

In Baptism we all die. The person who is a descendent of Adam, and is therefore subject to the curses of Adam, dies. We drown that person in water. We enter into Christ's death, his Crucifixion, as Saint Paul says, so as to take part in his Resurrection:

> Are you unaware that we who were baptized into Christ Jesus were baptized into his death? We were indeed buried with him through baptism into death, so that, just as Christ was raised from the dead by the glory of the Father, we too might live in newness of life. For if we have grown into union with him through a death like his, we shall also be united with him in the resurrection. We know that our old self was crucified with him, so that our sinful body might be done away with, that we might no longer be in slavery to sin.... If, then, we have died with Christ, we believe that we shall also live with him.... Consequently, you too must think of yourselves as [being] dead to sin and living for God in Christ Jesus. (Rom 6:3–6, 8, 11)

Through Jesus' sacrifice, all those who trust in Jesus and volunteer to die in Baptism are reborn as other Christs (Col 3:11; Gal 2:19–20). In place of the old person is a new person, united to the resurrected Mystical Body of Christ, adopted into God's family, and who is therefore another son or daughter of God. Saint Paul compares our Baptism into this new life with Christ to a second creation (2 Cor 5:17), and the Holy Spirit, present in our souls after Baptism, gives us the renewed spiritual life from which he principally gets his title "Giver of Life." According to the Second Vatican Council's Dogmatic Constitution on the Church, *Lumen Gentium* (November 21, 1964), all those who are baptized share in Jesus' anointing as priest, prophet, and king (see 10–12)—each baptized Christian is another "anointed one," another Christ. That is why in the Rite of Baptism for Children, immediately after the Baptism itself, the new Christian is anointed with sacred chrism in order to make it clear that this new person is another *christos*, "anointed one," sacred to the Lord as a result of the child's death and resurrection in the sacrament.

All this imagery of renewal and restoration and rebirth and re-creation captures the dimension of mercy as powerful goodness that we have explored in earlier chapters, mercy as the lifting of up of what was fallen, the restoration of deficiencies, the removal of privations, the healing of what was wounded, the fixing of what was broken, the righting of what was wrong. By introducing us into Christ's resurrected Body, Baptism gives us a portion of Christ's covenant-based power to right wrongs, and, therefore, a portion of his responsibility.

In some people Christ's power manifests itself as particular gifts or charisms (Rom 12:6–8; 1 Cor 12:8–10). Others are called to certain charismatic offices (Eph 4:11–13; 1 Cor 12:28). But all the baptized have a responsibility to see that the Gospel spreads and that the needs of our neighbors are met through the works of mercy. Our priorities in this life after Baptism must become Christ's, because, as we saw, our wills have to be one with his.

The Mass Incorporates Us into Christ's Paschal Sacrifice

The word "incorporation" means that we are made "into a body," and so it is appropriate to refer to Baptism and the Eucharist as two sacraments of incorporation, as Pope Saint John Paul II wrote in his Encyclical Letter on the Eucharist in Its Relationship to the Church, *Ecclesia de Eucharistia* (April 17, 2003):

> Incorporation into Christ, which is brought about by Baptism, is constantly renewed and consolidated by sharing in the Eucharistic Sacrifice, especially by that full sharing which takes place in sacramental communion. We can say not only that *each of us receives Christ*, but also that *Christ receives each of us*. He enters into friendship with us: "You are my friends" (Jn 15:14). Indeed, it is because of him that we have life: "He who eats me will live because of me" (Jn 6:57). Eucharistic communion brings about in a sublime way the mutual "abiding" of Christ and each of his followers: "Abide in me, and I in you" (Jn 15:4). (22; italics in original)

The Eucharist is called "the Body of Christ," just as the Church is, so it only makes sense that the Church and the Eucharist are intrinsically connected. If in Baptism we enter into Christ's sacrifice, in the Mass we make that sacrifice present again, so as to enter into it once again.

In the Mass, the faithful are made into the Body of Christ to be sacrificed to the Father by the priest, who acts in the Person of Christ. This is a key theme of the third Eucharistic Prayer:

> Look, we pray, upon the oblation [sacrifice] of your Church and, recognizing [in this oblation] the sacrificial Victim [Jesus] by whose death you willed to reconcile us to yourself, grant that

we, who are nourished by the Body and Blood of your Son and filled with his Holy Spirit, may become one body, one spirit in Christ [cf. Eph 4:4; 1 Cor 12:12–13]. May he make of us an eternal offering to you.[1]

Christ is both the priest who offers the sacrifice and the victim who is sacrificed; in the Mass, the priest makes present Christ the High Priest, and the baptized faithful make present Christ the Victim. This is the teaching of the Second Vatican Council concerning all the faithful: "Taking part in the eucharistic sacrifice, the source and summit of the Christian life, [the faithful] offer the divine victim to God and themselves along with it" (*Lumen Gentium*, no. 11).[2] Christ's Body is on the altar on the paten and also in the congregation.

Pope Pius XII gave a long explanation of this in paragraphs 80–94 in his Encyclical on the Sacred Liturgy, *Mediator Dei* (November 20, 1947), pointing out that the priest at the Mass represents both the people and Christ so that through the priest the people are also offering Christ to the Father, and through the priest the people are also being offered to the Father as the Body of Christ. (He also points out how foolish it would be, therefore, to let your mind wander at Mass![3]) Our identification with the Body of Christ in the Paschal sacrifice of the Mass calls us to the imitation of Christ in our daily lives:

---

1   Excerpt from the English translation of *The Roman Missal* © 2010, International Commission on English in the Liturgy Corporation (ICEL).

2   Translation from *Vatican Council II: The Conciliar and Post Conciliar Documents*, vol. 1, ed. Austin Flannery (Northport, NY: Costello Publishing/Dublin, Ireland: Dominican Publications, 1998), p 362.

3   "All the faithful should be aware that to participate in the eucharistic sacrifice is their chief duty and supreme dignity, and that not in an inert and negligent fashion, giving way to distractions and day-dreaming, but with such earnestness and concentration that they may be united as closely as possible with the High Priest, according to the Apostle, 'Let this mind be in you which was also in Christ Jesus' (Phil. 2:5). And together with Him and through Him let them make their oblation, and in union with Him let them offer up themselves" (80).

All Christians should possess, as far as is humanly possible, the same dispositions as those which the divine Redeemer had when He offered Himself in sacrifice: that is to say, they should in a humble attitude of mind, pay adoration, honor, praise and thanksgiving to the supreme majesty of God. Moreover, it means that they must assume to some extent the character of a victim, that they deny themselves as the Gospel commands, that freely and of their own accord they do penance and that each detests and satisfies for his sins. It means, in a word, that we must all undergo with Christ a mystical death on the cross so that we can apply to ourselves the words of Saint Paul, "With Christ I am nailed to the cross" (Gal. 2:19). (81)

God's covenant with Jesus is extended to us because in the Mass we become Jesus the High Priest and Jesus the Sacrificial Victim; as the Body of Christ together with Christ the Head, we offer ourselves to the Father as a sacrifice. What the sacrifice of Christ earned back from the Father, the sacrifice of the Mass also earns for all those who participate in it. What the Father in justice owes to Jesus after his sacrifice, he also owes to all those who have been reborn as Jesus and who take part in that sacrifice.

Anointing of the Sick as Configuration to Christ's Passion

The Church teaches that the Anointing of the Sick confers on a sick person a configuration to Christ's Passion:

> By the grace of this sacrament the sick person receives the strength and the gift of uniting himself more closely to Christ's Passion: in a certain way he is consecrated to bear fruit by configuration to the Savior's redemptive Passion. Suffering, a consequence of original sin, acquires a new meaning; it becomes a participation in the saving work of Jesus. (*CCC* 1521)

The sacraments all confer on us a configuration to Christ, so that through him we can be reunited to God the Father. All the sacraments are thus manifestations of God's merciful and powerful goodness that reorder our souls to God. We can often overlook the Sacrament of Anointing of the Sick among the seven sacraments, in part because in our culture we want to marginalize sickness and old age and suffering and death. But "suffering clearly has a place in the Church of the crucified Christ," as one theologian put it,[4] and so it should have a place in the spiritual life of the Christian.

Anointing of the Sick is our Lord's powerful response to particular spiritual needs as we grow closer to death. What are these needs?

Fear of death. As death approaches, whether in the form of sickness or old age, we can become afraid. Jesus himself in the Garden of Gethsemane was afraid of his death. This is a natural human response, because death is evil, a result of the Fall. Death was not part of God's original plan for us in Eden, and instinctively we react negatively to the thought of death—we have a vestigial memory as part of the human race that this is not the way things ought to be.

Temptation to despair. The devil tries to take advantage of our fear of death by attacking our trust in God. Why does God let me be sick? Is he really there? Is he really loving? Despair can lurk in wait. Was all my life for nothing? Is this poor life all that there is? Often, we conceive of ourselves as strong and independent; sickness and old age rob us of independence and strength, and can attack our self-image. ("I do not want to be a burden.")

Suffering. Often our last days are marked by sickness and suffering and frailty. Our bodies are not right, and our

---

4   Father Colman O'Neill, O.P., as quoted in Romanus Cessario, "Anointing of the Sick: The Sanctification of Human Suffering," *Nova et Vetera, English Edition* 17, no. 2 (2019): 306.

spiritual life often suffers as well. Even the saintly Thérèse of Lisieux became cranky and impatient on her deathbed.[5] It is hard to control one's emotions and moods when one is suffering. It is hard to care about others when one is in pain.

Loneliness. The sick and elderly are often afterthoughts even in the lives of their families. People who believed that their vocation was to raise a family find that their families now have families and lives of their own. It is fatiguing to meet new people and invest in new relationships, and so many people at the end of their lives do not summon the energy to be social.

Lack of purpose. Often people at the end of their lives do not know why God has not taken them yet. What is the use of being alive when you cannot contribute anything with an ailing body and fading intellect?

Attachment to this life. We are to walk through this vale of tears as pilgrims on a journey to our true homeland. And yet, we can become very attached to the things of this world. We have things we want to accomplish, people we want to be with, experiences we want to have (a "bucket list"). Death threatens to take us away from the opportunity to do more in this life.

Anointing of the Sick is a specific channel of grace, of divine power and goodness, that responds to these needs.

The Second Vatican Council's Constitution on the Sacred Liturgy, *Sacrosanctum Concilium* (December 4, 1963), points out that anointing specifically configures us to Christ's suffering and death, through which Jesus transformed suffering from a punishment into a prayer (73). Saint Paul tells us that Jesus invites us to share in his suffering (Col 1:24) so that in our bodies we can participate in his Cross and in his

---

5   *The Story of a Soul: The Autobiography of St. Thérèse of Lisieux,* trans. J. Clarke (Washington, DC: Institute of Carmelite Studies, 1975), 265–67.

self-sacrificial love. If we truly understand that we are incorporated into the Body of Christ, then for us suffering becomes filled with meaning—we are conquering the devil, extending the Kingdom of God, winning converts, aiding the Church, helping souls out of Purgatory, cooperating in the redemption of the world, accomplishing all the works that Jesus' Cross accomplishes. Our physical deterioration makes us spiritually powerful, because God gives us new opportunities to unite our sufferings to Jesus' in the sacrifice of the Mass.

Thanks to our incorporation into the Body of Christ, all the baptized are united to one another in the Communion of Saints, and so we are not alone. Anointing strengthens our awareness of this spiritual reality: "The sick person ... though the grace of this sacrament, contributes to the sanctification of the Church and to the good of all men for whom the Church suffers and offers herself through Christ to God the Father" (*CCC* 1522). The whole Church, with the angels and the saints, accompanies the sick person in this sacrament.

As we grow in understanding of the Cross, we come to appreciate God's providential plan for our salvation. We see that this world is not worth loving with all our heart. Suffering and fragility help us become detached from our bodies and this life, reducing the temptations to be attached to things.

The theologian Louis Bouyer observes that the life of the elderly and sick has a certain analogy to religious life. For the religious, the vows of chastity, poverty, and obedience foster their detachment from family, possessions, and personal independence, the better to prepare them for how things will be in Heaven. Similarly, the elderly often find that they have become detached from their families, from possessions (What use is a fancy car or big house when you cannot drive or navigate stairs?), and from their independence.[6] In Pope Saint John Paul II's Post-Synodal Apostolic Exhortation on the Consecrated Life, *Vita Consecrata* (March 25, 1996), the pope teaches that the vows of the religious anticipate how we will all live in the Kingdom of Heaven, for "the consecrated life is a foreshadowing of the future Kingdom" (26); the grace of Anointing helps the elderly person be similarly prepared for the life to come.

Some theologians think that Mary's greatest spiritual act was not at the Annunciation, but rather at the foot of the Cross when she perfectly consented to the Father's will that her Son sacrifice himself (see Lk 11:28). It is hard to accept God's will sometimes, especially when it requires us to suffer. Anointing helps the sick person's will become perfectly aligned with God's will. In Pope Saint John Paul II's Post-Synodal Apostolic Exhortation on Reconciliation and Penance, *Reconciliatio et Paenitentia* (December 2, 1984), the pope writes that "the anointing of the sick in the trial of illness and old age and especially at the Christian's final hour is a sign of definitive conversion to the Lord and of total acceptance of suffering and death as a penance for sins. And in this is accomplished supreme reconciliation with the Father" who uses suffering to purify our love (27). Anointing helps us accept God's will for us, that we obediently persevere in our self-giving even as our energies decline. Saint Alphonsus Liguori wrote that perfect acceptance of the suffering God sends us and resignation before our own death so completely aligns our will to God's that we no longer need Purgatory, having purged our souls of attachment to sin while still in this life. Saint Alphonsus assures us that if we submit perfectly to the divine will in the face of our death, "we shall certainly save our souls and die the death of saints."[7]

Anointing is a sacrament of mercy because it removes defects in our spiritual life, it teaches us more profoundly and

---

6   See Louis Bouyer, *Introduction to the Spiritual Life*, trans. Mary P. Ryan (Notre Dame, IN: Christian Classics, 2013), chapter 7, esp. 210–11.

personally about the redemptive suffering of Christ, it invites us to enter into Christ's own mercy by offering our own sufferings for the good of the Church and the merciful redemption of the world, and it forgives our sins if Confession is not available.

"For the Forgiveness of Sins"

Anointing forgives our sins, says Saint James in his epistle.

> Is anyone among you sick? He should summon the presbyters of the church, and they should pray over him and anoint [him] with oil in the name of the Lord, and the prayer of faith will save the sick person, and the Lord will raise him up. If he has committed any sins, he will be forgiven. (5:14–15)

Every Sunday in the Mass we say that both Baptism and the Eucharist are "for the forgiveness of sins." At the Cross, at the moment of Jesus' priestly sacrifice, both blood and water come from his Sacred Heart, forever linking the sacrament of Christ's blood with the sacrament of Christ's "living water" (Jn 7:38). The Letter to the Hebrews connects the sprinkling of water in Baptism (10:19–22) with the sprinkling of blood of the victim over the people in the Jewish sacrifices (9:11–26; cf. Ex 24:8) to take away sins and to seal the covenant with God. Both sacrifices wash away our sins, but not because our sins are something extrinsic to us like dirt. That imagery might

---

7   Leading up to this assurance, he states, "At death all our hope of salvation will come from the testimony of our conscience as to whether or not we are dying resigned to God's will. If during life we have embraced everything as coming from God's hands, and if at death we embrace death in fulfillment of God's holy will, we shall certainly save our souls and die the death of saints." Saint Alphonsus Liguori, *Uniformity with God's Will* (Charlotte, NC: TAN Books, 2009), chapter 4.

make sense with water, but not with blood. When the book of Revelation says that the martyrs have their robes washed white by the blood of the Lamb (Rev 7:14), this is not meant to be a normal washing, as if the blood were liquid soap! Rather, it is the effect of Jesus' purifying sacrifice, which cleanses us in our consciences, by restoring our hearts and reconciling us to God (Col 1:20) through the New Covenant.

Both sacraments are instruments of God's mercy, but it is important for us not to separate the forgiveness of sins from what we have been discussing regarding our incorporation into the Body of Christ. Baptism is not an act of leniency, but of covenant. Baptism forgives all the sins of the pre-baptized because their old selves die with Christ and their sins die with them (this is Saint Paul's argument in Romans 6:5–7). Reborn with Christ, the baptized begin their spiritual life anew. In Baptism, we are given the power to love God correctly because we now have the ability to love with Jesus' Sacred Heart, and not just our failed pre-baptized hearts (fulfilling the prophecy of Ezekiel 36:26: "I will give you a new heart"). That Baptism also forgives both Original Sin and personal sins is in some sense almost a side effect of this deep restoration of our souls. The sacrifice of the Mass "reinforces the incorporation into Christ which took place in Baptism though the gift of the Spirit (cf. 1 Cor 12:13, 27)" (*Ecclesia de Eucharistia*, no. 23).

As mentioned above, anointing also forgives our sins (Jas 5:15). As with Baptism and the Eucharist, this forgiveness of sins is something of a side effect of the deeper configuration to Christ's sacrifice. Because through the sacrament we are more perfectly united to Christ's sacrifice on the Cross, which heals our hearts and unites us to the sinless Son of God in the New Covenant, our sins are also forgiven.

Anointing does not replace Confession; the Church instructs priests that if it is possible to hear the confession of the person we are anointing (that is, if the person is conscious, lucid, and able to speak), we are supposed to do so before the anointing. That is part of the reason why it is a mistake to wait until the person is just about to die to call the priest— you want the sick person to go to Confession if possible. Furthermore, receiving the sacrament earlier allows the Church to respond earlier to the temptations and spiritual difficulties associated with the dying process. The whole sacrifice of Jesus and the whole New Covenant are about ending Original Sin, so these sacraments, which incorporate us into that, also forgive sins. To be configured to the resurrected Christ is to receive merciful healing.

12

The Tribunal of Mercy

God, the Father of mercies, through the death and resurrection of his Son has reconciled the world to himself and sent the Holy Spirit among us for the forgiveness of sins; through the ministry of the Church may God give you pardon and peace.

— Formula for absolution in the Rite of Penance

On Easter Sunday, Jesus breathed on the apostles, giving them both the Holy Spirit and the power to absolve sins (Jn 20:19–23). From the second-grade girl who walks out of First Reconciliation with a big smile on her face to the middle-aged man who is brought to tears over his lifetime of sins, through the Sacrament of Confession the vast majority of Catholics find the most concrete expression of God's mercy in their lives. As we have seen, the Sacrament of Confession is only one of the sacraments of God's mercy. It is ordered toward Baptism, in the sense that it restores us to the state of grace that we receive in Baptism. And it is also ordered toward the Eucharist, as part of our spiritual preparation to be able to receive the resurrected Lord.

Removing a Burden, Forgiving a Debt

Once we have been incorporated into Christ's sacrifice and thus into his covenant of mercy, we can still find our hearts drawn to our former way of life, as a "dog returns to its own vomit" (2 Pet 2:22). We can put our hands to the plow and then look back (Lk 9:62). We can fail to put away our old earthly self and its practices (Col 3:5–9). We can find within ourselves a carnal part warring against our spiritual desires (Rom 7:14–23). In other words, even though we are sons and daughters of God, we still find sin attractive. And when we sin after Baptism, we lose some of the effects of Baptism. After our Baptism, we once again become able to love God with charity, not simply because God does good things for us, but because he is "all good and deserving of all our love." In sinning, in choosing something that we think is better than obeying God, we re-create the damage to our hearts that the grace of our Baptism had healed. So, we need further healing.

In the Bible, sin is typically described using two different metaphors: a weight that must be borne, and a debt that must be paid. The scapegoat on the Day of Atonement would bear the burden of Israel's sins out into the desert, prefiguring how Jesus would bear the weight of our sins (1 Pet 2:24; Heb 9:28). The parable of the unforgiving steward compares our state of sin to someone with a debt so large it is unpayable (Mt 18:21–35). The debt language makes the theology of mercy easier to conceptualize: a debt is a kind of privation, and so the removal of a debt is a removal of a privation, which restores you to your original state. The idea that the penance assigned should in some way be proportionate to the sin stems from this theology that one is repaying or giving back what one owes.

But while credits and debts are abstract—the language of accountants—carrying a heavy weight is a primitive and visceral experience. My observation (as a priest who hears confessions) is that, for most people, the dominant feeling upon leaving the confessional is that of a weight having been lifted from them. And the graver the sin, the heavier it weighed (*gravis* in Latin means "heavy"; the word "gravity" comes from the same root). We can even combine the metaphors, so that someone "labors under the burden" of debt, which "weighs" upon him and can even be "crushing."

Having a weight lifted off our shoulders and a crushing debt relieved certainly is a powerful way of describing having our sins forgiven. And just as we appreciate it when someone carries something heavy for us, so we can feel gratitude for the whole team (Jesus, the Church, and the priest) that removed the weight of our sins from us.

The weight metaphor also emphasizes God's strength, that he can lift burdens which we cannot. Sometimes people will wonder what is the worst sin one can commit. Young people usually guess sexual sins, because those are the mortal sins most tempting to them. Some people suggest abortion or murder: sins against human life and dignity. Some think sins against God, such as sacrilege or apostasy. But God is strong enough to lift these sins from our shoulders, so all these are forgivable. In fact, God is strong enough to lift the weight of any sin we ask him to lift, so the only sin that he cannot forgive is the one we never ask him to.

The Council of Trent employed a third metaphor when it said that the priest giving absolution to a penitent is similar to a judge pronouncing a sentence in a tribunal. Pope Saint John Paul II, while not contesting this point, noted how this reveals the paradoxical nature of divine justice. In Confession, just as in a criminal court, a person is under judgment by a judge, the judge's role is to apply the law to this particular case, and the judge has to pronounce a sentence. But in court, if the accused pleads guilty, the judge imposes a sentence of "guilty." In Confession, on the other hand, if the penitent pleads guilty, the priest's sentence is, I absolve you! So while the confessional is a genuine tribunal, it is of an unusual sort: "a tribunal of mercy". As Pope Saint John Paul II observed in his Post-Synodal Apostolic Exhortation on Reconcilia-tion and Penance, *Reconciliatio et Paenitentia* (December 2, 1984), "According to the most ancient traditional idea, the sacrament [of Confession] is a kind of judicial action; but this takes place before a tribunal of mercy rather than of strict and rigorous justice, which is comparable to human tribunals only by analogy" (31).[1]

The Medicine of Mercy

According to the Code of Canon Law,

> In hearing confessions, the priest is to remember that he is equally a judge and a physician and has been established by God as a minister of divine justice and mercy, so that he has regard for the divine honor and the salvation of souls. (can. 978 §1)

There is another tradition in the Church, however, which regards Confession not just as a way in which sins are for-given, but as a way in which souls are healed—and this introduces yet another metaphor for mercy. The *Catechism* considers Confession to be a "sacrament of healing," along with Anointing of the Sick. The Code of Canon Law reminds the priest that he is "equally a judge and a physician." Pope Saint John Paul II writes in *Reconciliatio et Paenitentia*, "As [the Church] reflects on the function of this sacrament [of

---

1   See also Saint Faustina Kowalska, *Divine Mercy in My Soul: The Diary of the Servant of God Sister M. Faustina Kowalska* (Stockbridge, MA: Marian Press, 2008): "Write, speak of my Mercy. Tell souls where they are to look for solace, that is, in the Tribunal of Mercy [the Sacrament of Reconciliation]. There the greatest miracles take place and are incessantly repeated. ... Oh how miserable are those who do not take advantage of the miracle of God's mercy!" (1448). (Paragraph numbers, not page numbers, are used for all citations. Hereafter cited as *Diary*.)

Confession], the church's consciousness discerns in it, over and above the character of judgment ... a healing of a medicinal character" (31).

In the Middle Ages, people began to talk about the spiritual life having three basic stages: the purgative stage, in which one tries to purge one's life of mortal sin and the tendency to selfishness; the illuminative stage, in which under the light of grace one struggles against subtler sins and vices, and strives to make progress in virtue and in generosity; and the unitive stage, in which one becomes so identified with Christ's will that one looks with Christ's eyes and loves what he loves.

The weight and debt metaphors work very well to explain the value of Confession in the purgative stage, in which one's sins are heavier. But when someone comes to Confession with smaller sins, those metaphors do not make as much sense. I can carry small pebbles and small debts indefinitely, without much anxiety. For those in the illuminative stage of the spiritual life, then, it can make more sense to think of Confession as healing medicine.

This medicinal side of the sacrament reflects the restorative aspect of mercy, which we have emphasized in talking about Baptism. It comes to the fore especially when someone comes to Confession frequently, whether because a person sins repeatedly in one area or because he comes to Confession as part of a broader spiritual plan of life. Someone with an addiction to pornography or someone who frequently falls into a critical spirit toward the defects of his or her spouse comes to Confession to ask for the grace of the sacrament each time he or she falls, the way one might put ointment on a wound repeatedly until it heals. Confession brings us both pardon and peace. The medicinal side of the sacrament especially gives us the later grace, the grace of healing and peace.

Confession Reconciles Us with the Church Community

In the 1970s and 1980s, there was a movement in the Church to replace individual private Confessions with public penance services that involved a general absolution. The ambition of some of the reformers was to make penance services the norm, claiming that this was the way that things had been in the Church previously. Instead, according to the Code of Canon Law, the Church permits general absolution only rarely, and requires all those who receive general absolution to make an individual Confession at the first opportunity (cann. 961–63). These same reformers then pivoted to encouraging hybrid penance services, in which a group of people gather together for penitential prayers, then make their individual and private Confessions, and after return to the group for a closing prayer. In my experience as a priest, these never seem to work, nor are they very popular—most people leave when they finish their individual Confessions rather than reassemble for the final blessing, indicating that they simply regard the "service" part of the penance service to be extra and unnecessary. But the reformers keep wanting to push these things on parishioners. What are they trying to accomplish?

It might be the case that the Sacrament of Confession has undergone more changes throughout its history than any other sacrament. For example, in the early Church, penance preceded absolution, while today it is the other way around. In the early Church, absolution was reserved for the bishop, and necessary only for the most serious and public sins: apostasy, murder, and adultery.

The early Church tended to regard Confession as analogous to a kind of second Baptism and so created parallels between the two sacraments. Some of the liturgy surrounding Confession was based on the baptismal liturgy. The Church treated penitents analogously to catechumens, even to the point of absolving them of sins only during the Triduum. Those who confessed to the bishop one of those major sins would join what amounted to a religious order, the Order of Penitents, modeled after the Order of Catechumens—the latter of which is the precursor to our RCIA (Rite of Christian Initiation of Adults). Catechumens and penitents would both wear special habits to Mass, would sit apart from the main congregation, and would not receive Holy Communion. One could be "sentenced" to the Order of Penitents for several years or even for life (although these sentences could be reduced by an indulgence such as making a pilgrimage, the origin of the later practice).

The parallels with the catechumenate also extended to how the rest of the Church treated the penitents. Just as in our RCIA today, the faithful of the local Church would accompany the catechumens on their journey to Baptism by praying with them. As the Order of Penitents developed, it became the practice that the local Church community would similarly accompany those in the Order of Penitents on their journey to absolution. Since those in the Order of Penitents were usually to be absolved at the end of Lent on Holy Thursday or Good Friday, it became traditional that throughout Lent the whole congregation would accompany the penitent in solidarity by adopting penitential practices privately, taking on a portion of their penance through the Communion of Saints. Then, they would welcome back the penitent with joy before receiving the Eucharist together. This seems to have been the origin of Lent as primarily a penitential season for the whole Church—as fewer people were baptized as adults, the penitents greatly outnumbered the catechumens, and so the focus of Lent stopped being the preparation of the catechumens for Baptism, and instead became the local Church accompanying the penitents on their journey of reconciliation. Many of the Church's later practices regarding Purgatory also came from this tradition of the community sharing in the penance of the penitents: if the penitent died before completing his time in the Order of Penitents, the community could complete the penance for him through their private prayers, sacrifices, and indulgences.

This brings us back to our contemporary reformers. As scholarship became aware of this ancient practice of Confession, the reformers realized that the Church in the twentieth century had lost the sense of community that marked the ancient Church. Just as they successfully recovered something of the Order of Catechumens in the form of the modern RCIA, so they wanted to bring back some version of the ancient practice where a group of penitents confess their sins publicly and are publicly reconciled with the Church. Hence the move for general absolution. The Church has declared general absolution to be a (generally) bad means, but toward a very good end. That is because a key goal of the Sacrament of Confession is indeed reconciliation with the Church.

Despite the secrecy of its contents, Confession is never a strictly private affair. The priest represents the Church, so reconciliation with Christ in Confession is also a reconciliation with the whole Church. The theology of the Communion of Saints is that the good deeds and the sins of each member of the Church help or hurt the Church everywhere—the Body of Christ gets healthy or sick as an organic whole (1 Cor 12:26). So when a sinner is absolved in Confession, the whole Body of Christ gets healthier. That all happens invisibly and mystically. But the reformers are correct that there is room for more visible community involvement as well. For example, the whole parish should pray for all those who fall into sin and should offer sacrifices and mortifications to help sinners complete their journeys to reconciliation. I am not sure that penance services are the right way to manifest our solidarity with sinners; the logistics of modern life make them cumbersome events. Perhaps parishes could promote devotions such as the Chaplet of Divine Mercy or the use of the Fatima Prayer in the Rosary, or borrow from the communal penance practices of Lent for use during the rest of the year. But Divine Mercy is a public event that should be publicly celebrated. There is rejoicing in Heaven when one sinner repents; the penitent's neighbors on earth should rejoice as well.

Penance, Satisfaction, and Mercy

Saint Pope John Paul II teaches,

> Satisfaction is the final act which crowns the sacramental sign of penance. In some countries the act which the forgiven and absolved penitent agrees to perform after receiving absolution is called precisely the penance. (*Reconciliatio et Paenitentia*, no. 31)

In the Sacrament of Confession, we perform a penance. In the modern rite, this penance happens after the absolution, while in the ancient Church it preceded absolution. It is important to note that this penance is not a form of retributive punishment, but rather an act of satisfaction. The distinction between punishment and satisfaction and its use in theology originates with Saint Anselm of Canterbury.[2] In punishment something is taken from you by force, while satisfaction is a voluntary gift of something that is not taken. Satisfaction's purpose is to make up for the disorder that your sin caused to society by giving voluntarily something beyond what you took by sinning. Think of Zacchaeus the tax collector in the Gospel, who not only repaid the people he defrauded, but repaid

---

2   See Anselm, *Why God Became Man* (*Cur Deus Homo*), 1.11.13–14.

them four times over and additionally gave half his money to the poor (see Lk 19:8). Satisfaction is meant to reconcile one with the community offended by one's sin; it manifests one's contrition and conversion; it proves that one's will is no longer opposed to the law that was broken.

To make satisfaction, one must have the ability to give back more than you took. That is not always possible. Sometimes the disorder of your sin is greater than your ability to make it right. Saint Anselm argued that the disorder caused by Original Sin made satisfaction by human beings impossible. What could we give to God that could be more than what we took from him in sinning? We always owe him our very existence. To make satisfaction, we would have to give him everything we are, and then something else on top of it. That is not possible for any created being. As we saw earlier, Jesus was able to give satisfaction to God by offering his life, and then the Father, now in debt to Jesus, made satisfaction back to him by creating a New Covenant with Jesus and all those who are resurrected with him in Baptism.

We cannot possibly do enough in penance to make satisfaction for the sin we commit, as Pope Saint John Paul II reminds us in *Reconciliatio et Paenitentia*: "What is the meaning of this satisfaction that one makes or the penance that one performs? Certainly it is not a price that one pays for the sin absolved and for the forgiveness obtained: No human price can match what is obtained, which is the fruit of Christ's precious blood" (31). Because of this, the tendency of the Church in recent centuries is to move away from harsher or more elaborate penances (such as the yearslong penances of the ancient Order of Penitents mentioned earlier). In the same paragraph the pope continues,

> Acts of satisfaction—which, while remaining simple and humble, should be made to express more clearly all that they

signify—mean a number of valuable things: They are the sign of the personal commitment that the Christian has made to God in the sacrament to begin a new life (and therefore they should not be reduced to mere formulas to be recited, but should consist of acts of worship, charity, mercy or reparation). They include the idea that the pardoned sinner is able to join his own physical and spiritual mortification—which has been sought after or at least accepted—to the passion of Jesus, who has obtained the forgiveness for him. They remind us that even after absolution there remains in the Christian a dark area due to the wound of sin, to the imperfection of love in repentance, to the weakening of the spiritual faculties. It is an area in which there still operates an infectious source of sin which must always be fought with mortification and penance. This is the meaning of the humble but sincere act of satisfaction.

Longer penances are sometimes for the penitents' good; someone who has been away from the Church for a long time might be asked to spend a significant amount of time in prayer, talking with our Lord and restarting the relationship that has been neglected. But the purpose of the penance is not to undo the past, but to make the Church stronger by making the penitent's spiritual life stronger.

Public Sins and Public Penance

One purpose of the ancient practice of public penance was to make public satisfaction to the community so that everyone knew that you had turned your back on your sinful behavior and never wanted to sin again. This made sense particularly since public penance dealt with sins that were especially public: apostasy, murder, and adultery. Today, some quarters clamor for the Church to punish or otherwise sanction politicians who support abortion or some other policies against the moral law. They often reason that this would have a deterrent effect, but as we have seen, the real justification for such punishment should primarily be (1) the good of the politicians' souls constrained by (2) the good of the public order of the Church.

Few bishops have taken this course of action, often preferring to do nothing or to permit the politician simply to go to Confession and make private penance. This gets the satisfaction wrong. Private penance makes satisfaction to God, "saying" that you are sorry by suffering in solidarity with Christ's suffering. In the case of public defiance of Church teaching, which does public damage to the Church's pastoral efforts and spiritual life, satisfaction must also be made to the local Church. Because the sin is public, the satisfaction also ought to be public in some form, to signify publicly the politician's contrition. Only then should the local Church welcome back the politician. It is more pastorally difficult to demand that a powerful person denounce his sin and make public penance. Rather than repent, he might retaliate, as Henry II did to Saint Thomas Becket. But mercy must promote good order and justice. Because sins are much greater when influential people commit them publicly, the satisfaction must be greater as well.

13

Justice, Mercy, and the Spiritual Life

From the beginning of the Church until today, there have been people who emphasized the Church's strict standards of justice and her call to perfection, and others who have emphasized the grace and mercy of God toward sinners. The first party accuses the second of laxity; the second accuses the first of rigorism. In the early Church, the fight was about what to do with apostates, those who under the Roman persecutions had sacrificed to pagan gods. In our day, the debates might be about the divorced and civilly remarried, or how strictly to enforce the Church's sexual morality. But almost all the disagreements about spirituality in our day bear the scars of the great fight between rigorists and laxists known as the Jansenist controversy, which lasted in one form or another from the seventeenth century until Vatican II and perhaps even until today. And in some ways, at the center of the fight is the spiritual disease known as scruples.

Treating Pebbles like Boulders

We have seen that the Bible uses a set of metaphors that treats sin as a weight to be borne. I once heard someone use this weight metaphor to explain why we should organize our confessions by confessing the weightiest sins first. Imagine you were to walk some great distance with a boulder on your shoulder and also a dozen pebbles in your pocket. When you arrived where you were going, the normal thing would be to put down the boulder first and then to discard the pebbles. In the same way, one should organize one's confession to tell the heaviest sins first, before the venial sins.

Some people, however, are so sensitive about sin that they feel every pebble as if it were a boulder. This is the origin of the term "scruples," which comes from the Latin word for pebble (*scrupulus*). Scruples is a spiritual disease in which one is so anxious or obsessive about offending God that one believes with little or no reason that one has condemned oneself to Hell. This frequently arises from a mistaken idea of God's justice wherein the scrupulous person thinks God is primarily interested in condemning him.

Scrupulous people are often very committed to the study of moral and spiritual doctrine, but with the perverse effect that their study makes them know all the ways that they fail to be perfect, and they despair of ever going to Heaven. Scrupulous persons are often proudly egotistic, desiring to impress God with their perfect obedience—which is ultimately a form of self-love—rather than simply to love him with all their heart. They are almost always stubborn with their confessors, and often critical of them for not being strict enough.

Scruples often comes in the form of doubting, for no good reason, whether past Confessions were valid: someone "does not feel forgiven" or worries that he was not completely contrite, or thinks he failed to explain himself well enough, and so needs to start over. This is yet another example of treating pebbles like boulders: if a person has tried to make a good Confession, even if the past Confession was imperfect in one of these details, it would not make the Confession invalid. And a valid Confession in which one has confessed all mortal sins in number and species absolves not only those mortal sins but also venial sins, though confessing the latter is recommended (see Council of Trent, Session 14, chapter 5; see also *CCC* 1458).

Jansenist Rigorism versus Mercy

The rigorist spiritual tradition known as Jansenism for several centuries taught that all sins were like boulders. Jansenists saw having a soul sensitive to the slightest imperfection and deeply sorry for the smallest sin as a virtue and a sign of sanctity. It was everyone else who had the spiritual disease of lukewarmness. One of the goals of the Council of Trent was that people would receive Communion more frequently. A century after Trent, the Jansenist theologian Antoine Arnauld argued that Communion had become too frequent, that consciences had become too lax, and that therefore sacrilege toward the Blessed Sacrament was common.

Because the Sacrament of Confession prepares one for receiving Communion, frequent Confession also became more and more common after Trent. After hearing penitents confess the same sins as before without any moral progress, the Jansenists argued that there needed to be a change in how easily absolution was being granted. They urged a return to the practice of the early Church, in which those who had committed sins would wait years until their absolution, but they wanted a more medicinal purpose to the penance: rather than have a sentence of a determinate length of time, they wanted people to become perfectly detached from all sin before they could be absolved from their sins and receive Communion. The Jansenists held a high standard for holiness, the standard of having our wills completely united and subservient to Christ's. They promoted the justice of God and preached fiery sermons about the condemnation to Hell awaiting those who fell short of God's justice. They believed that God's justice was primarily retributive, that God in his justice needed to punish sinners and not forgive them, but that his justice could be placated by punishing someone else in place of the sinner. The idea that one person could substitute for another is a cousin of Protestant "penal substitution" theories of the atonement; the Catholic twist was that through the Communion of Saints spiritual elites could allow God to punish them in place of the actual sinners. This self-sacrificial suffering by saints on behalf of sinners created a kind of solidarity that compensated for the great differences in holiness between the saints and sinners. There was thus a kind of indirect mercy in Jansenism, the strong taking the blow intended for the weak. But Jansenists were skeptical of those who preached that God was other than retributive in his punishment. They feared that, as a pastoral practice, to preach mercy was to preach leniency and laxity (a common critique of mercy, as we have seen).

The Defense of God's Mercy in Theology

The Church responded to this rigorist tendency with a flowering of reflections on mercy and its relationship to justice, perhaps reaching its peak in the theology of Saint Alphonsus Liguori, the great eighteenth-century moral theologian and Doctor of the Church. As a youth influenced by Jansenist spirituality, Saint Alphonsus developed tremendously harmful scruples, constantly worrying that he had sinned subconsciously, that his fallen humanity made him deaf to the whispers of the Holy Spirit in his soul, that he had failed to communicate to his spiritual directors and confessors just how sinful he really was so that their advice and penances were too lax. Suffering from such torment of soul forced Saint

Alphonsus to think his way out of his scruples by understanding the true relationship of justice and mercy.

Saint Alphonsus agreed with the tradition of the Church that true holiness involved complete submission to God's will, and his sensitivity of soul made him aware of the myriad of subtle ways in which human self-love could turn one away from the path of righteousness. But he also preached that it was not enough to conceive of holiness as not sinning. Alphonsus wrote copiously instead of God's mercy and love, how Christ's Passion revealed the unshakeable truth that God loved the world and loved each of us, that it was out of love that God sent his Son, and that God's mercy was more powerful than our sins.

In theological manuals for confessors and popular devotionals and everything in between, Alphonsus developed a spirituality that called everyone to the highest standards of justice while at the same time encouraging those who fell short that God was a Father who loved them and whose grace would help them. He wrote several treatises in particular on how to deal with scruples, which for most people are curable through good theology of God's mercy and good formation from a trusted spiritual director.

The Defense of God's Mercy through Popular Devotion to the Sacred Heart

In the meantime, the pastors of the Church responded to Jansenism with divinely inspired creativity.

In 1675, the Jesuit priest Saint Claude Colombière, the newly assigned spiritual director to the Visitation nuns at Paray-le-Monial, was asked to speak to a nun, Margaret Mary Alacoque, who claimed she was having visions of Jesus, and that Jesus was asking her to spread devotion to his Most Sacred

Heart throughout the whole Church. Saint Claude realized that this devotion could be very useful in the fight against Jansenism as a way to teach people to trust in God's mercy.

The heart of Jesus has been an object of devotion ever since the soldier at Calvary pierced it with a lance, fulfilling the prophecy of Zechariah that the Messiah would be pierced (Zech 12:10). Saint John calls attention to this dramatic moment among the many dramatic moments of the Passion by doubling down on his credentials as a witness: "An eyewitness has testified, and his testimony is true; he knows that he is speaking the truth, so that you also may [come to] believe" (Jn 19:35). Thanks to such literary attention to one scene, devotion to the heart of Jesus soon followed. The physical heart of Jesus as an object of devotion symbolizes also the fact that Jesus is the incarnation of the love of the Father. God sent us Jesus because he loved the world (Jn 3:16); it was from the Father's love that the Son became flesh and dwelt among us in the flesh (Jn 1:14). Since the heart is both a human organ and the metaphorical seat of human love, devotion to the Sacred Heart is an aspect of devotion to the humanity of Jesus. And because Jesus' humanity was instrumental in our salvation, the great act of divine mercy, devotion to the Sacred Heart is a devotion to Jesus as Mercy Incarnate.

The details of the devotion as revealed to Saint Margaret Mary were perfect counters to Jansenism. While Jansenism thought that people should rarely receive Communion, devotion to the Sacred Heart involved receiving the Eucharist on the first Friday of each month (which counted as frequent by the standards of the day). And while Jansenism involved a level of detachment from the world that was better suited to angels, the Sacred Heart emphasized Jesus' humanity, his human heart with which he loved both us and his Father. The devotion pays special attention to Jesus' Passion as a sign of his merciful love. Saint Margaret Mary stated that Jesus wanted her to spend a "Holy Hour" every Thursday night to meditate on his agony in the Garden of Gethsemane. Devotees were to mortify themselves in solidarity with Jesus' sacrifice on the Cross and make reparations with their prayers and sacrifices on behalf of those whose sins, even today, were the cause of his great suffering for us. The devotion asks us to respond to Jesus' sacrifice for us with our own sacrifices, taking on some portion of his redemptive suffering (see Col 1:24) so as to share in the price he paid for the sins of the world. Responding to love with love, sacrifice with sacrifice, mercy with mercy, Catholics with a devotion to the Sacred Heart grew in their love of Jesus and also learned to love with Jesus' heart all those he loved.

The devotion that Saint Margaret Mary's visions detailed emphasizes God's mercy while at the same time avoiding presumption and spiritual laxity. Basically, nobody who is aware of Jesus' pierced and suffering heart can have anything other than a hatred of the sin that made it necessary. Nonetheless, Jansenists hated all this talk about Jesus' physical heart being the incarnation of God's love. They referred to devotees as "heart idolaters,"[1] and fought against the spread of the feast of the Sacred Heart.

Thérèse of Lisieux and the Consecration to Divine Mercy

Another divinely inspired antidote to Jansenism can be found in the spirituality of another French nun, Saint Thérèse of Lisieux. Thérèse was also affected by scruples as a young girl and was spiritually over-sensitive for years, until God's grace healed her and infused her with a magnanimity that could

---

1   Timothy T. O'Donnell, *Heart of the Redeemer* (San Francisco: Ignatius Press, 1992), 151.

not be constrained by the simple goal of "not-sinning." She wanted to love everything and everyone with Jesus' love.

Some nuns in her convent, under the influence of a Jansenist reading of Carmelite spirituality, decided to make a spiritual offering to God's justice. In typical Carmelite spirituality, one is aware that holiness is a process that moves through stages. Those who are further along these steps are closer to a state of spiritual union with God than those who are further away. The Jansenist interpretation that attracted some Carmelites encouraged these self-consciously elite souls to show mercy to the non-elites through the Communion of Saints, by asking God to give them all the retributive punishment he was going to give to sinners and give the sinners all the merits they had earned as faithful religious. They called this a consecration to divine justice.

Thérèse reacted negatively when she heard about this. In response, she decided to make a consecration of herself to God's mercy, asking that she be overwhelmed and purified by "the fires of God's love." Rather than offering God her perfection, painstakingly acquired after years of spiritual work moving through the various stages of the spiritual life, she preferred to offer God her whole being, despite it being very imperfect and very little (her offering to God would be her "empty hands," she declared in her act of consecration). God did not need to wait for decades of spiritual work to make her holy. If he wanted, he could make her holy instantly; like a father carrying his little girl in his arms, God could pick her up and take her to the top of the staircase, skipping all the "steps" of the spiritual life.

Her serious insight, couched in the imagery of being a spiritual child, was that by making herself little and humble she depended on God to make her holy through his abundant grace (his mercy). By eschewing a picture focused on God's severity, she did not abandon penance and sacrificial suffering for others—she simply suffered for love, for the same reason Jesus did, who loved so much that he hurt when others suffered.[2] Jesus commanded us to love, not merely to avoid sin.

In an earlier chapter, we noted that recent theology tends to identify mercy with God's love, while the earlier theology of Saint Thomas sees mercy as an aspect of God's powerful goodness. That change is almost certainly a reaction to Jansenism's image of God's severe and angry justice. As much as anyone, Saint Thérèse's writings and letters helped form ideas about spirituality, justice, and mercy in the first half of the twentieth century and brought God's merciful love to the foreground.

God's Love as an Excuse for Spiritual Laxity

It would take another book to describe all the reactions to Jansenist ideas about justice in the Church over the last centuries. The legacy of Jansenism left its mark on the spirituality of the Church, even through to the Second Vatican Council. As evidence of this, nearly every pope between the First and Second Vatican Councils wrote an encyclical promoting devotion to the Sacred Heart. And Saint Pius X, who did not write an encyclical, instead promulgated the First Friday devotion to the Sacred Heart throughout the universal Church. After Vatican II, however, a segment of the Church thought that rigorism, and in particular scruples, was still a great spiritual threat. Influenced by the prestige of psychotherapy, many spiritual writers in the era of the Council began to look at Freud's critique of "repression," saw in it an analogy to the spiritual

---

2   Saint Thérèse of Lisieux, *Story of a Soul*, 3rd ed., trans. John Clark (Washington: ICS Publications, 1996), 180–81 (Manuscript A, 84 [recto], 3–84v [verso]. 9); her act of consecration to divine mercy is on pp. 276–77. See also, Michael E. Gaitley, *33 Days to Merciful Love* (Stockbridge, MA: Marian Press, 2016), especially 69–84.

disease of scruples, and over time came to regard almost the entirety of traditional Catholic spiritual practices as contributing to scruples.

In 1972, the Jesuit spiritual director George Aschenbrenner wrote an influential article criticizing the practice of examining one's conscience. The daily examination of conscience is a practice that goes back to the Desert Fathers and was a mainstay of the spirituality of Saint Ignatius of Loyola, the founder of the Jesuits. But, Aschenbrenner wrote, examination of conscience "has narrow moralistic overtones.... Its prime concern was with the good or bad actions that we had done each day."[3] Rather than focusing on things that we have done wrong, Aschenbrenner wrote, we should instead focus on "God's revelation, a steadfast love in Christ Jesus always inviting and invigorating our consciousness."[4] His goal was to move us from judgmental "conscience" talk to love-centered "consciousness" talk.

The Desert Fathers thought that tears over one's sins could be a charismatic gift of the Holy Spirit, but for Aschenbrenner, contrition only adds happy notes of "body and depth" to our spiritual "song of deep joy and gratitude." Our examination of consciousness leads us to "wonderful sorrow" when we recognize our "lack of honesty and courage in responding to God's call." Contrition is "a faith experience as we grow in our realization of our dear God's awesome desire that we love God with every ounce of our being."[5] Sin is redefined as dishonesty, or as failing to respond to God's calling us to sing with him, but not as disobedience to God's will. There

---

3   George Aschenbrenner, *Quickening the Fire in Our Midst: The Challenge of Diocesan Priestly Spirituality* (Chicago: Loyola Press, 2002), 167. Aschenbrenner's first article on this theme originally appeared under the title "Consciousness Examen" in *Review for Religious*, January 1972, 14–21.

4   Aschenbrenner, *Quickening the Fire in Our Midst*, 188.

5   Ibid., 175–76.

is no concern for objective criteria of good and evil, because that would be "juridical" and lead to scruples. Saint Ignatius believed that evil spirits could try to tempt him to sin, and so in classic Jesuit spirituality the "discernment of spirits" meant discerning whether my spiritual impulses come from God or the devil (see 1 Jn 4:1). For Aschenbrenner, the spirits are simply "interior experiences" in which a person either does or does not "find himself being his true, congruent self in Christ." The spiritual battle with the forces of darkness was replaced with self-discovery.

Aschenbrenner was by no means the worst of the 1970s spiritual writers, and for that reason he has remained influential until quite recently. His aversion to talking about justice, law, order, evil, and punishment in favor of talking exclusively about God's love is instead typical of the last half-century. He probably thought he was saving the Ignatian practice from neglect, as the whole culture was pivoting toward therapy and away from talk of duty and order. His worry throughout his reformulation of Ignatian spirituality was that the traditional practice of examining one's conscience—namely, looking back at what one had done during the day, being thankful to God for one's spiritual successes but contrite for one's sins and defects, and finally resolving to do better tomorrow—would lead people to scrupulosity and rigorism, to unhealthy mental states, and even to depression.

The correct response to errors about God's justice, however, is not to make the equal and opposite errors regarding God's mercy. As we have seen repeatedly, justice is not retribution and strictness, nor is mercy leniency. The response to Jansenist rigorists is not to embrace laxity; the Jansenists were right to reject laxity. The correct response is to teach the truth: that God's standard for us is spiritual perfection, perfect obedience to God's will; that our Baptism makes this possible so long as we cling to God's grace; that Jesus' sacrifice on the Cross is more powerful than any sin of ours; and that God sends us suffering and trials as a way of forming us so that his punishment is primarily medicinal, and actually reveals his fatherly love for us.

From Frequent Confession to No Confessions

In 1905, Pope Pius X tried to put an end to Jansenist controversies about Communion. He decreed that all the faithful should go to Communion frequently, even daily; that "no one who is in the state of grace, and who approaches the holy table with a right and devout intention" could be denied access to Communion; and that the criteria of "state of grace" and "right and devout intention" were pretty easy to meet.[6] As the twentieth century progressed, more and more people went to Communion frequently. Many people also started coming to Confession extremely frequently so as to receive the Eucharist worthily when they did. They kept the traditional association between Confession and Communion and increased the frequency of both.

This trend created an unexpected set of problems. Confessors were faced not just with longer lines, but also with the unusual problem of what to say to someone who comes to Confession as often as each week. The practice of frequent Confession and Communion had previously been restricted to religious orders, and in those cases over the centuries the

---

6   "A *right intention* consists in this: that he who approaches the Holy Table should do so, not out of routine, or vainglory, or human respect, but *for the purpose of pleasing God, or being more closely united with Him by charity, and of seeking this Divine remedy for his weaknesses and defects....* It is sufficient that they [the daily communicants] *be free from mortal sin*, with the purpose of never sinning in future. ... Care is to be taken that Holy Communion be proceeded by serious preparation and followed by a suitable thanksgiving, according to each one's strength, circumstances, and duties." Decree of the Sacred Congregation of the Council, "De quotidiana SS. Eucharistiæ sumptione" (December 20, 1905), quoted in "Frequent Communion," by Thomas Scannell, in *Catholic Encyclopedia*, vol. 6 (New York: Robert Appleton, 1909) (italics added), https://www.newadvent.org/cathen/06278a.htm.

practice had developed to treat Confession as an opportunity also for spiritual direction. The religious penitent would not just confess major sins, but also venial sins, tendencies to vice, thoughts and temptations toward sin, and even mere defects in love. At times, Confession became indistinguishable from spiritual direction so that it was thought important always to go to the same confessor for spiritual direction. The Church took this model for Confession-as-spiritual direction and scaled it up so that it became part of the vocation of every diocesan priest-confessor to give spiritual advice to those who received the sacrament frequently. Diocesan seminaries added classes on spiritual theology, and theologians wrote books to help confessors think like spiritual directors.[7]

Pope Pius XII strongly defended the practice of frequent Confession against critics in his Encyclical on the Mystical Body of Christ, *Mystici Corporis Christi* (June 29, 1943):

> It is true that venial sins may be expiated in many ways which are to be highly commended. But to ensure more rapid progress day by day in the path of virtue, we will that the pious practice of frequent confession, which was introduced into the Church by the inspiration of the Holy spirit, should be earnestly advocated. By it, genuine self-knowledge is increased, Christian humility grows, bad habits are corrected, spiritual neglect and tepidity are resisted, the conscience is purified, the will strengthened, a salutary self-control is attained, and grace is increased in virtue of the Sacrament itself. Let those, therefore, among the younger clergy who make light of or lessen esteem for frequent confession realize that what they are doing is alien to the Spirit of Christ and disastrous for the Mystical Body of our Savior. (88)

---

7   Two important examples include Adolphe Tanquerey's *The Spiritual Life: A Treatise on Ascetical and Mystical Theology*, and Benedict Bauer's *Frequent Confession: Its Place in the Spiritual Life*.

Pius XII's account of the benefits of frequent Confession are manifestly true. But the fact that "the younger clergy" in the 1940s were already undermining the practice suggests that its days were numbered.

Some scholars think that the seeds of the current crisis were sown already in the decree of Pope Saint Pius X about frequent Communion. By making the standards of Communion so low, they argue, it meant that people would often receive our Lord without having recently gone to Confession. In previous generations, one *felt* a certain way when receiving Communion, because one had gone to Confession immediately beforehand. After a few decades of receiving Communion without having that feeling, the connection between the two sacraments was lost for many people.

The decree of Pope Saint Pius X intended to balance Jansenist rigorism. But its success, along with the successes of all the other ways the Church fought Jansenism, created a different spiritual climate, and what had been balanced started to wobble. Today, after fifty years of "Jesus loves you" laxity, things have fallen completely the other way. In today's context, so few people worry about God's justice or sin that they tend to presume on his love. The correct response is not a neo-Jansenist revival, swinging back to rigorism. It is preaching the truth, that we must obey God's will as perfectly as possible, but out of love, and that we must sacrifice ourselves for others, also out of love.

A serious attention to God's love for us ought to provoke us to sorrow when we fail to love God back; Aschenbrenner was not wrong about that. But we must remember that attention to rules and commandments and all the other aspects of justice is a requirement of love. As Jesus said to the apostles, "If you love me, you will keep my commandments" (Jn 14:15). Some people are on the purgative stage and need to be reminded of the dangers of sin more frequently; others are at the illuminative stage and need to be exhorted to greater generosity in their spiritual life. There ought always to be tension in the spiritual life, at whatever stage, because we always must be offering everything we have, including our lives, to God and for those he loves (see Jn 15:12–13).

14

Devotion to Divine Mercy

Despite the misunderstandings regarding mercy characteristic of our time, many people have become interested in mercy because of Catholic feasts and devotions. Pope Saint John Paul II instituted the feast of Divine Mercy and canonized Saint Faustina Kowalska in the year 2000. Pope Francis has made mercy a theme of his pontificate since his first public appearances after his election, in his papal motto, and especially in his proclamation of the year 2016 as the Extraordinary Jubilee Year of Mercy. Before that, the Church has promoted liturgical feasts promoting devotion to the Sacred Heart of Jesus, to Mary's Immaculate Heart, to the Cross, to the Precious Blood of Jesus, to divine intercession in various key moments in history (as in the feast of Our Lady of the Rosary), and for a whole class of saints (such as Saint Vincent de Paul) who practiced works of mercy.

Petitions for God's mercy and prayers of confidence in Divine Mercy are part of every Mass, from the beginning Confiteor-Kyrie sequence ("I confess to Almighty God ... Lord, have mercy") through the Eucharistic Prayers making God's sacrifice of mercy present again, to the Agnus Dei ("Lamb of God, who takes away the sins of the world"), to the Domine Non Sum Dignus before Communion ("Lord, I am not worthy to have you enter under my roof ..."), to receiving Communion itself as the meal that seals the Christian covenant. Because so many Catholics understand God's mercy by way of the liturgy and popular devotions, we will examine some features of the most popular devotions to God's mercy.

Lex Orandi, Lex Credendi

When Pope Saint John Paul II published the third secret of Fatima in 2000, he invited Joseph Cardinal Ratzinger, the prefect of the Congregation for the Doctrine of the Faith (and future Pope Benedict XVI), to give an official "theological commentary" on the revelations at Fatima. It is a brilliant piece of theology, which deserves to be better known. Cardinal Ratzinger comments,

> Popular piety is a sign that the faith is spreading its roots into the heart of a people in such a way that it reaches into daily life. Popular religiosity is the first and fundamental mode of "inculturation" of the faith. While it must always take its lead and direction from the liturgy, it in turn enriches the faith by involving the heart.

Attending Mass is necessary to go to Heaven, says the Church. But it is not enough. "The spiritual life ... is not limited solely to participation in the liturgy," says the Second Vatican Council in paragraph 12 of its Constitution on the Sacred Liturgy, *Sacrosanctum Concilium* (December 4, 1963). Devotions, while they cannot supplant the Mass or the sacraments, are an important part of our spiritual life as Catholics. They are not just for the uneducated, as some snooty people may assert. Saint John Henry Newman evangelized the English upper classes and intellectuals by promoting tasteful (rather than kitschy) Catholic devotions that appealed to the affective side of our human nature. Even though Catholic popular piety can at times become imbalanced, the Church values the depth of commitment it adds.

The word "devotion" has its root in a Latin word for love, and it would be a mistake to uproot or overregulate ways that people foster a love for God and for his people. When approved by the Church, devotions are pastoral instruments that promote certain virtues or remove certain vices, that fight heretical theologies and help us worship God correctly. *Lex orandi, lex credendi* is a slogan of the ancient Church—"the law of prayer is the law of belief." And so, when someone comes to the Church with a mistaken idea or caught in a cycle of bad thinking, correct devotions are very useful.

In our day, in which our social media and our political discourse are so judgmental and critical in spirit, I am grateful as a priest and shepherd of souls for the many devotions in the Church promoting God's mercy. It is a shortcut in preaching or Confession to be able to appeal to phrases or hymns or prayers that people already know, which can help reorient them on the right path to God. To those who confess anger toward another person, I can assign as a penance the Chaplet of Divine Mercy to ask God's blessings on the person and encourage them to pray for the grace to look on the person with God's merciful eyes. For those who have scruples, thinking that God wants to send them to Hell, praying the Stations of the Cross can remind us how much God is willing to do out of love for us. For those suffering from lukewarmness, contemplating the Sacred Heart of Jesus can lead them to aspire to spiritual greatness while avoiding perfectionism, fostering a desire to help alleviate the sufferings of Christ by taking some small part of the sufferings ourselves.

There are complex theological principles that are communicated effectively through these popular devotions, and the Church would be foolish not to use them. The form and content of these devotions, however, needs to be corrected by the Church at times, because bad devotions can lead people away from the Faith. In the fourth century the Church entirely banned the use of singing at Mass for a time, because the Arian heretics had written such popular liturgical hymns that people were humming along with heresies. In the year 1613, the Holy See instructed the Carmelites to stop preaching that wearing the brown scapular would get you out of Purgatory the Saturday after you died ("the Sabbatine privilege"), an idea which misrepresented what sacramentals are and how Purgatory works. Again, *lex orandi, lex credendi*. Devotions are powerful teachers, and their lessons should lead people closer to Christ.

The Status of Special Revelation regarding Devotions to God's Mercy

Three devotions to Divine Mercy popular in our day all have a certain prestige that comes from their being the results of what the Church calls "private revelation" (*CCC* 67). I refer to the devotion to Divine Mercy as promoted by Saint Faustina, the devotion to the Sacred Heart as promoted by Saint Margaret Mary Alocoque, and the devotions surrounding the apparitions at Fatima—namely, devotion to the Immaculate Heart of Mary and the so-called Fatima Prayer ("O my Jesus, forgive us our sins, save us from the fires of Hell . . .") often added to the Rosary. These devotions have an exalted status because Jesus or Mary appeared to a particular saint or saints to inspire them to promote this devotion, and the Church has approved these revelations and even added feasts to the liturgical calendar based upon them.

It happens, however, that some Catholics can hold mistaken convictions about these devotions, and when they do, they may also hold mistaken ideas about mercy and justice. If our

Lord or our Lady says something, then that is more important than what the bishops or popes say, right? If the "institutional" Church does not exactly obey what some visionary says God told her, then so much the worse for the Church. At one parish where I served, one parishioner—a dear old man with deep and sincere piety—insisted that Saint Faustina's diaries were equal in importance to the Bible because Jesus himself had dictated portions to her!

In his theological commentary on the message of Fatima previously cited, Cardinal Ratzinger suggested that the name "revelation" given to private revelations is something of a misnomer, because it gives the impression that it is basically the same as the "public" revelation, "which finds its literary expression in the two parts of the Bible: the Old and New Testaments" and "has reached its fulfilment in the life, death and resurrection of Jesus Christ." The Church teaches that revelation of God to man is complete with the death of the last apostle. Cardinal Ratzinger, in the same commentary, speaks to this: "In Christ, God has said everything, that is, he has revealed himself completely, and therefore Revelation came to an end with the fulfilment of the mystery of Christ as enunciated in the New Testament." The Church sometimes calls this the "deposit of faith," to signify that God left everything we need to know in a deposit that we guard (see 1 Tim 6:20; 2 Tim 1:14).

Private revelations, by which the Church means "all the visions and revelations which have taken place since the completion of the New Testament," are not at all like that definitive revelation. It is not as though the only difference was that one was public and the other was private; rather, "the two realities differ not only in degree but also in essence." One is the object of faith; the other is merely a help to faith. That does not mean that private revelation is worthless. Far from it. It contributes to a deeper appreciation of the mysteries of

God and his plan. It responds to the needs of a particular time and place. It helps by calling attention to certain aspects of the faith and, Cardinal Ratzinger writes, "can be a genuine help in understanding the Gospel and living it better at a particular moment in time; therefore, it should not be disregarded."

The Church approves a private revelation when it determines that it can be helpful and direct people back to Christ and the Church. The approval has a very specific meaning:

1. "The message contains nothing contrary to faith or morals;
2. "it is lawful to make it public; and
3. "the faithful are authorized to accept it with prudence.... It is a help which is offered, but which one is not obliged to use."

Private revelations, then, are clearly of a lower status than the Bible and are less essential to the spiritual life of the faithful than attending Mass on Sundays, confessing one's sins at least annually, supporting the Church financially, and all the other precepts of the Church listed in the *Catechism* (2041–43). Those are obligations, minimum requirements for getting to Heaven. The Church is clear that private revelations are not at that level.

Modern-Day Prophecy

What private revelations are, Ratzinger argues, is modern-day prophecy. Not prophecy in the sense of predicting the future, but prophecy in the sense of the Old Testament: "Prophecy in the biblical sense does not mean to predict the future but to explain the will of God for the present, and therefore show the right path to take for the future." In the Old Testament, the prophets would tell the people that the way they were practicing the Faith was not in accordance with God's will. In the Gospels, John the Baptist did the same (especially to Herod and Herodias). Some members of the charismatic movement have made the point that prophecy is routinely listed as one of the gifts of the Spirit (1 Cor 12:28–29; Eph 2:20; 3:5; 4:11; Rom 12:8), and so one would not expect it to disappear altogether. Ratzinger agrees: "In every age the Church has received the charism of prophecy, which must be scrutinized but not scorned." Saint Paul over and over speaks of prophecy being a key manifestation of the Holy Spirit, one which must be examined by the Church: "Do not quench the Spirit. Do not despise prophetic utterances. Test everything; retain what is good" (1 Thess 5:19–21).

Ratzinger's insight is that private revelations fall into the same biblical category. Recall that we said the revelations to Saint Margaret Mary Alacoque about devotion to the Sacred Heart seemed perfectly suited to respond to the Jansenist heresy. If we think of her as a prophet, we can see that she is manifesting the will of God in her time, and thereby leading the people of that time into a deeper understanding of what the Faith already teaches. Thinking of these private revelations as prophecy and their recipients as prophets might make us even more likely to think they are obligatory for us. After all, ignoring the warnings of the prophets never went well for Israel. But, Ratzinger continues, unlike with the inspired writings of the New Testament evangelists, these prophetic graces are received only imperfectly, because their content is beyond the capacity of the prophets to understand and articulate.

The visions do not actually change the way light strikes the eye of the visionary; the words do not make sound waves that strike the ear. Instead, they affect the mind and soul in some mystical way. They are not like "photographs" of Heaven;

rather, they are interior perceptions of realities that are beyond the senses, which need to be "translated" to be understood.

These translations are affected by the limitations of the recipients. Ratzinger uses the example that child visionaries like those at Fatima (and also Lourdes or La Salette) do not have the spiritual vocabulary to be able to explain precisely what they saw, and so they resort to images that they try to describe to others. In some cases, the simplicity of the visionaries helps give credence to their visions; there was no way that Saint Bernadette knew anything about the doctrine of the Immaculate Conception, for example, so nobody believed that the words she attributed to the Lady were made up. But that simplicity also means that their interpretations of what they saw might be in some way partial or limited. Even adult prophets cannot always understand everything they "see," as with the prophets in the Old Testament, who sometimes revealed more than they knew (such as the prophecy of Emmanuel in Isaiah 7:14). This is why even when the Church approves the visions as real, the devotions that come from them may need to be adjusted in order to be in accord with correct doctrine and practice.

Thinking of private revelations as in the biblical category of prophecy also helps us understand why visionaries are not necessarily holy, or perhaps better, why holiness is an achievement different from being a visionary. Saint Paul exhorts the Corinthians to strive not for the gift of prophecy but for the greater spiritual gifts of faith, hope, and, above all, love (1 Cor 12:31—13:2). Ratzinger calls attention to the classic warning of Saint John of the Cross, quoted in the *Catechism*: "Any person questioning God or desiring some vision or revelation would be guilty not only of foolish behavior but also of offending him, by not fixing his eyes entirely upon Christ and by living with the desire for some other novelty" (65, quoting Saint John of the Cross, *The Ascent of Mount Carmel*,

II, 22). The example of Jonah, who was an effective prophet but hardly a holy man, reinforces this point.

The grace of prophecy is for the building up of the people of God, for the holiness of others, but not the prophet's own holiness. Personal holiness requires the gift of charity. The two spiritual gifts are different, which means that when the Church canonizes a visionary, she is making a statement about the visionary's life of charity, and not adding the visions to the Church's canon.

The Devotion to Divine Mercy and Its Understanding of Justice

When I first read the diaries of Saint Faustina, I was nervous about the picture of God they presented. Similar to what we saw earlier in the case of Saint Thérèse, in the diaries, God's mercy is placed in opposition to the concept of God's justice, understood in Jansenist fashion as a wrathful desire to punish sinners in the name of retribution. Saint Thérèse's rejection of that Jansenist image of divine justice was instinctual, and (as far as I can tell) she never subscribes to it herself. Saint Faustina's diaries, on the other hand, not only assume that the Jansenist idea of justice is correct but actually appropriate that false idea of divine justice to the person of God the Father. In the first volume of her diaries, for example, she says that Jesus revealed to her that the Father's anger was being held back by Jesus' mercy and the souls who pray to it: "The prayer of a humble and loving soul disarms the anger of my Father" (*Diary*, no. 320). If taken at face value, this would imply the heretical view that the persons of the Trinity might have opposing wills.

The more I read her diaries, the less worried I became. She does not think that God the Father is without mercy, or that the Trinity is divided over whether to punish or forgive sinners (see, for instance, no. 1073). Faustina was not a theologian, and her diaries are not written with theological precision or with an eye toward publication. The descriptions of God her visions provide are not always consistent. She frequently hears Jesus appeal to the Jansenist idea of justice as retributive punishment, as when he explains to her, "My mercy does not want this [the suffering of the souls in Purgatory] but my justice demands it" (no. 20). Jesus gives Faustina different reasons to explain why she suffers on earth. At one moment it is because of retributive justice ("You are guilty of one day of fire in purgatory" [no. 36]); a few pages later, she hears that she suffers in atonement for the sins of others (no. 39); and later, in her brilliant description of the dark night of the spirit, she understands her suffering as a spiritual purification (nos. 95–106).

There also seems to be some development in her understanding of mercy over the course of her life, so that retributive punishment seems more prominent a theme toward the beginning of her diaries and seems less prominent by the end (although, in no. 1146, God describes a door of lenient mercy and a door of threatening justice). If we were to try to parse Faustina's locutions as if they were the inspired writings of Saint Paul, rather than a soul in prayer trying to make sense of mystical phenomena, there would not be a possibility of any sort of development or deepening of understanding over the course of Faustina's life. If the idea were that she was just writing down the words Jesus dictated to her, then her personality would not matter, her understanding of what she heard would not matter, her limitations in education or holiness would not matter. But if Ratzinger is right, then all those things do matter.

Saint Faustina's diaries frequently speak of how she learned and grew over time, how she needed purification and greater dedication to prayer. By her own admission, she was a better vessel of God's graces as she matured (see no. 1318). The end of her diaries focus less on punishment and much more on expiation and sacrifice, on the communion of graces in the Body of Christ, on Faustina identifying her sufferings with Christ's on the Cross, on the evil of not trusting in God or not turning to him when in need, on the importance of fighting lukewarmness in the spiritual life and at Mass, on how the message of mercy will help those afraid of God or suffering from scruples, on obedience and humility to her spiritual director, on the need for the prayer of spiritual union. Her prayer experiences at the end of her life are often focused on increasing her charity and union with God, which one would expect from a soul that has passed through the illuminative stage of spiritual growth to the unitive stage. God never relaxes his desire that she give herself entirely or that she be perfect, but his message of mercy fights against any and all temptations to fear imperfection as a sort of failure.[1] These later parts of her diaries are especially deep and fruitful.

Devotion to Divine Mercy within the Church

The Church has canonized Saint Faustina and has promoted a devotion to God's mercy along the lines of her revelations, especially by renaming the Sunday after Easter as Divine Mercy Sunday and attaching indulgences to those who take part in prayers and devotions to Divine Mercy organized in the parish or who say the Creed, the Our Father, and an aspiration to God's mercy while praying in front of the Blessed

---

1 For example, no. 1578: "Let souls who are striving for perfection particularly adore My mercy.... I desire that these should distinguish themselves by trust in my mercy.... I will provide them with everything they will need to attain sanctity [*i.e., rather than having to earn them through merits*].... On the other hand, I am sad when souls ask for little, when they narrow their hearts."

Sacrament. In doing so, the Church does not mention Saint Faustina by name or quote from her writings or even mention the Divine Mercy Chaplet or novena,[2] and even encourages pastors on Divine Mercy Sunday not to focus on Saint Faustina but on the Easter mysteries themselves.[3] The Church permits the publication of Faustina's diaries as of spiritual value for the faithful, but it does not require that theologians accept the vision of Purgatory from the eighth day of the novena to Divine Mercy, nor the theological implications of any particular locution. Her writings have tremendous value, but not authority.

To sum up, it is permissible to have disagreements with individual parts of Faustina's diaries, and to want to clean up even some of her reported locutions, while at the same time believing those locutions to be objective mystical phenomena and prayer experiences, and thinking she is a saint. The devotions for Divine Mercy Sunday, as approved by the Church, are directed not to the visions of Faustina but rather to the mercy of God itself.[4] As such, they do not present any theological questions at all.

---

2   Apostolic Penitentiary Decree on Indulgences Attached to Devotions in Honour of Divine Mercy (June 29, 2002), http://www.vatican.va/roman_curia/tribunals/apost_penit/documents /rc_trib_appen_doc_20020629_decree-ii_en.html.

3   Congregation for Divine Worship and the Discipline of the Sacraments, *Directory on Popular Piety and the Liturgy* (December 2001), *Devotion to the Divine Mercy*, no. 154. "In connection with the octave of Easter, recent years have witnessed the development and diffusion of a special devotion to the Divine Mercy based on the writings of Sr. Faustina Kowalska who was canonized 30 April 2000. It concentrates on the mercy poured forth in Christ's death and resurrection, fount of the Holy Spirit who forgives sins and restores joy at having been redeemed. Since the liturgy of the Second Sunday of Easter or Divine Mercy Sunday—as it is now called—is the natural locus in which to express man's acceptance of the Redeemer's mercy, the faithful should be taught to understand this devotion *in the light of the liturgical celebrations of these Easter days* [italics added]. Indeed, the 'paschal Christ is the definitive incarnation of mercy, his living sign which is both historico–salvific and eschatological. At the same time, the Easter liturgy places the words of the psalm on our lips: "I shall sing forever of the Lord's mercy" (Ps 89[88] 2)' (John Paul II, encyclical letter *Dives in Misericordia*, no. 8)," http://www.vatican.va/roman_curia/congregations/ccdds /documents/rc_con_ccdds_doc_20020513_vers-direttorio_en.html.

4   In this, the Church follows the way it has long treated devotion to the Sacred Heart of Jesus, focusing more on Jesus' heart and sacrificial mercy than the visions of Saint Margaret Mary. See *Directory on Popular Piety and the Liturgy*, nos. 166–72.

Divine Mercy and the Signs of the Times

Cardinal Ratzinger says that visions and locutions are prophecies that respond to the signs of the times (see Lk 12:56). We already discussed how the devotion to the Sacred Heart did this, by providing a response to Jansenism. The devotion to Divine Mercy promoted by Saint Faustina has been growing since World War II, but it really blossomed thanks to the efforts of Pope Saint John Paul II, even becoming a part of the liturgical calendar at the beginning of this century. What may be the signs of our times to which this prophecy and devotion are a response?

As we discussed in an earlier chapter, ours is an era of anger. Our politics runs on anger, and the politicization of more and more of society makes us angrier and angrier. We get so angry at those who commit injustice or who have the wrong political opinions that we cannot even talk to them. We dehumanize them, call them names, and wish them ill. We only associate with people like us; we only read the blogs and watch the shows of those with whom we agree. In our day we tend to have no desire to understand or show solidarity with those on the other side.

That habit of anger bleeds over into personal life. We hold on to resentments. We promise to love our spouses every day of our lives and then criticize and criticize until we decide our differences are irreconcilable. We celebrate anger as making us stronger, as a way of standing up for ourselves and giving us dignity in the face of those who disrespect us. We get angry when we are slighted and feel righteous about being angry.

The devotion to Divine Mercy helps to combat this. The devotion teaches us to pray for those who are sinners, to call God's blessings down upon those who we think are doing wrong. Praying the Divine Mercy Chaplet or the novena puts into practice one of Jesus' more difficult commands—"Love your enemies, and pray for those who persecute you"—and moreover teaches us to pray for the right reason, "that you may be children of your heavenly Father, for he makes his sun rise on the bad and the good, and causes rain to fall on the just and the unjust" (Mt 5:44–45). We enter into the mercy of the Father as his children, showing mercy to those he loves and striving to look on them as he does.

Not only is praying for those in need of God's mercy itself a work of mercy, but it also teaches us to think in a Christian fashion about those who fall short of God's standards, regarding them with solidarity rather than condemnation, working in cooperation with God for their conversion and salvation. Jesus died for sinners, and to follow Christ, we should unite our will to his by desiring their conversion and salvation.

15

Works of Mercy

One of the common mistakes people make is to identify mercy with being lenient, with not punishing someone with the full severity of the law. But, as we have seen, mercy is not the opposite of justice. Rather, it should be thought of as restoring justice and right order to people's situations and their souls when they have become wrong and disordered. This broader conception of mercy helps makes sense of a tradition in the Catholic Church of calling things like almsgiving, feeding and housing the poor, educating people in the Faith, and holding funerals "works of mercy." If mercy were defined as merely not punishing, it could not explain why burying the dead is a work of mercy. But if we think of mercy as righting a wrong, of lifting up those who have fallen, of restoring all those in society (as much as is possible) to the place they should be were the world not fallen, then we should think that, of course, helping the poor is an act of mercy.

All the dimensions of mercy are required of us—not merely in the sense of having a merciful or benevolent heart, but in doing actual deeds (i.e., works) that come from such a heart.

What Are the Works of Mercy?

Saint Thomas Aquinas gives us the traditional list for the works of mercy:

Seven corporal works of mercy are posited, viz., (a) feeding the hungry..., (b) giving drink to the thirsty..., (c) clothing the naked..., (d) sheltering the homeless..., (e) visiting the sick..., (f) ransoming the captive..., and (g) burying the dead....

Likewise, seven spiritual works of mercy are posited, viz. (a) instructing the ignorant..., (b) counseling the doubtful..., (c) comforting the sorrowful..., (d) correcting the sinner..., (e) forgiving the one who offends us..., (f) bearing burdens and wrongs ..., and (g) praying for everyone. (*Summa Theologiae* II–II, q. 32, a. 2)[1]

Saint Thomas organizes these all under the category of almsgiving (*dare eleemosynam*), which he defines as "a work by which something is given to someone who is needy out of compassion because of God" (*Summa Theologiae* II–II, q. 32, a. 1).

Works of mercy are works, not just good intentions. They involve gifts given to someone who is needy, not to an equal as in other forms of gift exchange; as we have seen, this requires that the giver be in the relevant respect superior to the receiver. The gifts are given not out of self-interest but out of compassionate solidarity for the person in need. And if they are true works of mercy, they are given because of a love of God, who especially loves those in need.

The Works of Mercy Remedy Basic Human Needs

You can see that the traditional list always specifies someone who is "needy" (*indegenti*): the hungry, the thirsty, the

---

1   Translation is from the *New English Translation of St. Thomas Aquinas's* Summa Theologiae, by Alfred J. Freddoso, updated January 10, 2018, https://www3.nd.edu/~afreddoso/summa -translation/Part%202-2/st2-2-ques32.pdf.

ignorant, the sinner, the captive, the dead, and so on. This traditional list of works of mercy is not meant to be exhaustive but simply to indicate the types of human neediness (what we called "privations" earlier) to which we can respond.

Aquinas divides the needs of the body into several categories. Everybody has certain bodily needs, which can be divided into inner needs (such as the need for solid food and liquid food) and exterior needs (such as for clothing and a place to live). From this division comes the corresponding works of mercy: feeding the hungry, giving drink to the thirsty, clothing the naked, and giving shelter to those who need it. In addition, some people have specific or particular privations, which can be interior needs like a particular disease, or exterior needs like being captured. The corresponding works of mercy are visiting the sick (to help them and minister to their needs, not just to say hi) and ransoming the captive.

Saint Thomas acknowledges there are many needy people who do not fit into these categories. This list does not mention blindness, for example, or being lame and needing help to walk, let alone being poor—all of which are classic biblical categories for the needy. It mentions ransoming the captive, which was more common in earlier eras with different forms of warfare, but not visiting the person in prison (which is often included in modern lists of the works of mercy). We often today consider helping the elderly to be an act of charitable service, but being old is not the same as being sick or being in prison. That is why Aquinas thinks his categories are more helpful than the exact list:

> All other needs are reduced to these, for blindness and lameness are kinds of sickness, so that to lead the blind, and to support the lame, amount to the same as visiting the sick. On like manner to assist a man against any distress that is due to an extrinsic cause comes to the same as the ransom of captives.

> And the wealth with which we relieve the poor is sought merely
> for the purpose of relieving the aforesaid needs: hence there was
> no reason for special mention of this particular need. (*Summa
> Theologiae* II–II, q. 32, a. 2 ad 2)

So, if we can think of a person in any sort of serious bodily need, they can become objects of corporal works of mercy. It is the same with spiritual needs and spiritual works of mercy.

Works of Mercy Are Works of Charity

Saint Thomas' definition of almsgiving—again, "a work by which something is given to someone who is needy out of compassion because of God"—emphasizes not just the need that is to be remedied but also the motive of the person doing the almsgiving. One who performs a work of mercy must do it from mercy, acting out of compassion for the person in need and out of a love for Christ in that person. After all, Jesus criticizes those who give alms for other motives (Mt 6:1).

Saint Thomas argues that works of mercy arise from the supernatural virtue of charity, which, as Saint Paul teaches in his famous "Hymn to Charity" (1 Cor 12:31—13:13), is the greatest gift of the Holy Spirit. This leads Saint Thomas to a striking conclusion: "To give alms formally, i.e. for God's sake, with delight and readiness, and altogether as one ought, is not possible without charity" (*Summa Theologiae* II–II, q. 32, a. 1 ad 1). In other words, if a good deed is not done in cooperation with the Holy Spirit, out of a love for God that comes exclusively as a gift from God, and while in a state of grace, then it is not a work of mercy.

This is not a point that Catholic formation today emphasizes enough. A few years ago, one of my parishioners, who was a recent graduate of the University of Notre Dame and was a member of the local alumni association here in Boston, came to me with a concern. The previous weekend, he had taken a turn at the soup kitchen where the Notre Dame Club of Boston helps out from time to time. He said that the typical member of the alumni group of the nation's premiere Catholic university did not go to Mass or practice his faith but nonetheless was very eager to do acts of service to the poor. He wondered at this phenomenon, and rightly so.

Pope Francis, starting from the very beginning of his pontificate, has been trying to root out this attitude of separating works of mercy from the practice of the Faith. In a homily during one of his first Masses as pope, he said, "We can walk as much as we want, we can build many things, but if we do not profess Jesus Christ, things go wrong. We may become a charitable NGO, but not the Church, the Bride of the Lord" (Homily, March 14, 2013). He was echoing a sentiment Mother Teresa made many times in letters to her nuns: "You cannot have the vow of charity if you have not got the faith to see Jesus in the people we contact. Otherwise our work is no more than social work."[2]

There is a difference between Christian works of mercy and social work or work in the nonprofit sector or at a nongovernmental organization like Doctors without Borders or the Peace Corps. Those latter organizations can help lots of people with great efficiency and effectiveness, in genuinely important ways. But the help they give is limited. True works of mercy, that come from charity, are works of grace that reach into the hearts of both the needy person and the person who helps and that unite them both to Christ.

---

2   Mother Teresa, *Where There Is Love, There Is God*, ed. Brian Kolodiejchuk (New York: Doubleday, 2010), 158.

Works of Mercy Are Not Optional

According to Jesus, works of mercy are not optional:

> Depart from me, you accursed, into the eternal fire prepared
> for the devil and his angels. For I was hungry and you gave me
> no food, I was thirsty and you gave me no drink, a stranger and
> you gave me no welcome, naked and you gave me no clothing,
> ill and in prison, and you did not care for me. (Mt 25:41–43)

In the account of the Last Judgment (Mt 25:31–46), Jesus
tells those who are being condemned to eternal punishment that it was their failure to perform certain acts that
caused them to be condemned, and he tells those who are
ushered into the Kingdom of God that it was their performing
of these acts that caused them to be rewarded. These acts were,
significantly, performed uncalculatingly—those who fed the
hungry and clothed the naked and so on were not doing it
for any reward, while those who neglected to do so were not
aware that their neglect was being watched and judged (or
else, it seems, they would have acted differently in order to be
rewarded). Jesus thus makes it frighteningly clear that he wants
us to do certain things for one another, and to do them not
just for some external reward but because we want to. Saint
James, in a famous passage from his epistle, declares, "What
good is it, my brothers, if someone says he has faith but does
not have works? Can that faith save him? If a brother or sister
has nothing to wear and has no food for the day, and one
of you says to them, 'Go in peace, keep warm, and eat well,' but
you do not give them the necessities of the body, what good
is it? So also faith of itself, if it does not have works, is dead"
(Jas 2:14–17). Saint Paul makes similar points: "What matters
is keeping God's commandments" (1 Cor 7:19). Saint John is
blunt: "If someone who has worldly means sees a brother in

need and refuses him compassion, how can the love of God remain in him? Children, let us love not [merely] in word or speech but in deed and truth" (1 Jn 3:17–18). Works of mercy are essential for entering the Kingdom; good intentions by themselves do not suffice to save us.

The Gospel on Five Fingers

Jesus adds another layer to this requirement of salvation when he identifies himself with those who are in need, saying, "Whatever you did for one of these least brothers of mine, you did for me" (Mt 25:40). He would teach the same thing to Saint Paul on the road to Damascus, that to persecute Jesus' followers is to persecute Jesus himself: "He fell to the ground and heard a voice saying to him, 'Saul, Saul, why are you persecuting me?' He said, 'Who are you, sir?' The reply came, 'I am Jesus, whom you are persecuting'" (Acts 9:4–5). In other words, to help or neglect or persecute one of those given to Christ is to do the same to Christ himself. Mother Teresa calls this the Gospel on our five fingers. Writing to her nuns, she says, "Our work for the poor is so real, so beautiful because if our heart is pure, we can see, we can touch, Jesus twenty-four hours [a day] because He has made it so clear: 'Whatever you do to the least of my brethren—You—did—it—to—Me.' The Gospel in our five fingers."[3]

If our love for our fellow human beings is not enough motivation for us to help others, our piety and love of Christ should be. Mother Teresa makes a comparison between Christ's presence in the Eucharist and Christ's presence in the poor: "At the altar, how gently and tenderly the priest touches the consecrated host, with what love he looks at it. The priest believes

---

3 Ibid., 161.

that the host is the disguise of Jesus. Now in the slums, Jesus chooses as His disguise the miseries and poverty of our people in the slums."[4] If we are devoted to Jesus, we should also be devoted to the works of mercy. Devotions and prayers that help us to grow in our love of Jesus ought to fill our hearts with a love of Jesus in those who need mercy. To love Jesus is to love with his heart, to love those he loves. There can be no separation between our love of God and our love of neighbor. That is the five-fingered Gospel: "You—did—it—to—Me."

Philanthropy and Generosity

Aristotle makes a helpful distinction in his *Nicomachean Ethics* (4.1–2) between the type of generosity accessible to all people and the philanthropic works that only the very wealthy can accomplish. He describes philanthropy and generosity (sometimes translated as "magnificence" and "liberality") as distinct virtues, because there is a separate skill involved in figuring out how best to use one's riches for the common good compared with the disposition to be generous with only limited resources. To be sure, those who have more money than they need to supply all their necessities for the rest of their lives still have chances to be generous in areas other than money: with their time, for example, since for every person the day is twenty-four hours long; with their attention; and with their love.

The parable of the merciless steward (Mt 18:21–35) tells us that the command to be merciful applies to everyone, and not only to the very rich. No matter how far down the socioeconomic scale we are, we still have an obligation to be generous to others, and God will condemn us for failures in the works of mercy.

---

4   Ibid., 158.

His master summoned him and said to him, "You wicked servant! I forgave you your entire debt because you begged me
to. Should you not have had pity on your fellow servant, as I
had pity on you?" Then in anger his master handed him over
to the torturers until he should pay back the whole debt. (Mt
18:32–34)

Sometimes we can regard the poor as simply "takers" who
are objects of mercy and our charitable works but who themselves are not called to any sort of generous activity. Such a
view would dehumanize the poor. In my ministry as a col-
lege chaplain, I have accompanied students on mission trips
to impoverished places in Latin America. Over and over the
students realize how rich these impoverished communities
are in their charity toward one another. These people lack
necessities such as potable water, and yet they (more or less)
willingly give of their time to help their neighbors. The students sometimes will romanticize the way they rely on one
another, suggesting that it would be better that they remain
in poverty so that their interdependence not be corrupted
by American ideals of independence and self-reliance. That
is a mistake—we should strive to combine both a basic standard of living and care for our neighbor, rather than think we
have to pick only one. But that people can be misled in this
way should remind us that material poverty is often united to
great generosity.

The poor are called to spiritual greatness just as much as the
rich, which means that the poor are called to be generous and
merciful even as much as the greatest philanthropist. Even if
they do not have much to share in the ways of wealth, God
demands of them that they perform the other works of mercy:
comforting the sorrowful, correcting the sinner, forgiving the
one who offends, bearing with the defects and wrongs of others, praying, taking care of the feeble and infirm, making sure

that everyone is treated with dignity. Poverty is no excuse for being small-minded and turned in on oneself.

Works of Mercy Are Limited by the Demands of Good Order

There is also the question of how much we should help those in need. Jesus tells the rich young man to sell everything he has and give the proceeds to the poor. He praises the widow who gives her last money to the Temple. The theologian Gary Anderson points out that in doing this, Jesus moves beyond the rulings of the rabbis of his day, who had arrived at the conclusion that one should not give more than 10 percent of one's income in alms. Jesus, who gave his life for those he loved, commands his disciples to do the same: "This is my commandment: love one another as I love you" (Jn 15:12). So, it seems that we ought to exhaust ourselves and our resources to help others in need.

That is not wrong, but it is more complicated than that. The commandment to be as generous in our works of mercy as Jesus was generous in giving his life should be regarded within our earlier discussion of how mercy is related to a larger order-ing of people and things. Mercy is always in the service of God's just order, because mercy is about restoring those who are not in their proper place in that order to that proper place in God's plan for all creation.

Merciful assistance should be offered to all those who lack what they should have, until the point when doing so threat-ens due order. If it is possible for us to help someone in need so that he is no longer in need, we should do that, so long as we do not neglect our other duties and other people in need. It would be wrong, however, to help one poor person become rich, or one hungry person to become fat, when there are other poor or hungry people who could also be helped with those resources. It is usually better to give out a little at a time, rather than all at once. And lest we be falsely optimistic about our ability to solve the problems of human neediness, Jesus promises that there will always be more needy people so long as the world is fallen: "You always have the poor with you" (Jn 12:8).

Charity Begins at Home

We cannot save everybody; it is a theological mistake to try (and pride to think we can). Yet we can help particular people. How should we choose whom to help? The traditional answer is that our first responsibility is for the people we know or encounter directly. The Fathers of the Church saw it as part of God's providence that certain people who need help are placed before us; as Saint Augustine says in *On Christian Doctrine*:

> All men are to be loved equally. But since you cannot do good to all, you are to pay special regard to those who, by the accidents of time, or place, or circumstance, are brought into closer connection with you. For, suppose that you had a great deal of some commodity ... [that] could not be given to more than one person. If two persons presented themselves, neither of whom had ... a greater claim upon you than the other, you could do nothing fairer than choose between them by drawing lots ... Just so among men: since you cannot provide for all, you must provide for those who happen to be more closely associated with you, as if the question of whom to help were decided for you by lots. (1.28)[5]

5   Author's adaptation of the translation by James Shaw, in *Nicene and Post-Nicene Fathers*, 1st series, vol. 2, ed. Philip Schaff (Buffalo, NY: Christian Literature Publishing, 1887), revised and edited for New Advent by Kevin Knight, 2020, https://www.newadvent.org/fathers/12021.htm.

By helping those whom God has placed in our lives, we fulfill our part in the divine order to make this fallen world a little better.

This sort of thinking is especially true for our families. If we have a family and children, we should not give so much to charity that we must become beggars ourselves to support our family. In such a case, God has given us a particular responsibility for our family, such that it is our role in the divine order to provide for these particular people first. We should not neglect that responsibility, which effectively circumscribes and limits our almsgiving.

This way of thinking, however, must not become an excuse not to do anything. It is not a moral obligation to provide luxuries for your family, or to give your children every advantage so as to launch them into the next socioeconomic level. On the contrary, if we are aware of a neighbor in need and instead spend money on our families unnecessarily, we very well may be on the wrong side at the Last Judgment. We would be neglecting Christ himself. Most of us most of the time can help more than we do. We might not be able to help everybody, but we can help one more person make it through one more day.

Be Merciful as Your Heavenly Father Is Merciful

To be holy, we must identify our will with that of God the Father. That is our prayer in the Our Father, that God's will be done on earth (in our souls) as perfectly as it is in Heaven. Since Jesus' will is identified with his Father's, we will become holy if we identify our will with Christ's. Jesus' New Covenant comes with a new commandment, a new standard for loving: we are to love not according to the measure of our own hearts, but according to the standard of his Sacred Heart.

No longer do we love our neighbors only as much as we love ourselves, but we are to love one another as Jesus has loved us. Just as Jesus loved us more than he loved his own life, so we should love those around us more than we love our own time, comfort, pleasure, security, or plans for our future. Our money and all of our gifts and talents are not for us but for the restoration of God's Kingdom. As Jesus sacrificed himself for the redemption of the world, so we should sacrifice everything we have been given so that all might be saved and come to the knowledge of the truth. To offer everything for those Jesus loves: this is the measure of mercy for us on earth.

16

Mother of Mercy, Mirror of Justice

Our Lady is a great figure of mercy. That is partly because mercy is often associated with feminine and maternal qualities, with nurturing and consoling and encouragement. As we have seen, however, mercy requires not only a benevolent will but also the ability or power to make a difference to someone in need. Catholic devotion to Mary reflects this. Our devotion to Mary is not because she is a nice lady but because she is powerful enough that we can say in the Memorare that "never was it known that anyone who fled to your protection, implored your help, or sought your intercession was left unaided." Mary is powerful as well as kind, with a power that comes from her complete identification with her Son. It seems only appropriate that we end this book by considering our Mother of Mercy.

The Lowly Handmaid, Full of Grace

Long before Saint Thérèse offered to God's mercy her little self with her empty hands, Mary had already blazed the path of humility and littleness at the Annunciation: "Ecce ancilla Domini! Fiat mihi secundum verbum tuum." "Behold, I am the handmaid of the Lord. May it be done to me according to your word" (Lk 1:38).

Saint Thérèse wanted to empty herself of all pretense to holiness, rather than trying to show up at her particular judgment with a basketful of "merits" as some of her Jansenist-influenced sisters did. Saint Thérèse thought that by being little and empty, by giving away the "merits" her good deeds earned her for the benefit of others, God could fill her with his grace and make her holy.

Mary had already invented the spirituality of humility and emptiness when she told Saint Gabriel that she was "the handmaid" of the Lord, his servant or even slave girl, who would trust God to do with her in his loving providence whatever he intended. In the Magnificat (Lk 1:46–55), she continues on this theme: on her own, she is just the lowly handmaid, but her lowliness makes the Lord's action in her life that much more impressive. All generations will call her great and blessed, but that has nothing to do with her and everything to do with God's grace. If she were anything other than lowly and empty on her own, she could not be completely filled with God's grace. Therefore, her lowliness magnifies, gives testimony to, God's greatness and might.

The angel Gabriel's salutation to Mary—"Hail, full of grace" (Lk 1:28, RSV-2CE)—does not use her human name, but rather her name in Heaven. In the same way that "Michael" means "Who is like God?" and "Gabriel" means "God is my strength" and "Raphael" means "God heals," so Mary's name in Heaven is "She who is full of grace." Gabriel addresses her also as by the name Mary a few verses later ("Do not be afraid, Mary" [Lk 1:30]), because his use of her heavenly name was both puzzling and troubling. But from Heaven's perspective, the singular thing about Mary was that she was completely filled with God's grace.

We have pointed out that in order to be merciful, it is not enough to be well-intentioned, because we also have to be powerful enough to help. Mary's "power" is not her own but rather God's gift to her. Her superpower is, paradoxically, her lowliness and humility, that which provides God with a vessel for his grace that is so empty of pride and self-love that he can fill it completely.

Queen and Patron

One of the oldest Marian prayers invites us to fly to Mary's patronage, to present her with our petitions and our necessities, and to ask for her protection. All the saints in Heaven act as patrons and intercessors, presenting the prayers of the faithful on earth before God's altar in the heavenly Temple (see Rev 5:8). Mary's patronage as Queen Mother of the King of Kings would have been especially desirable: "Sub tuum praesidium confugimus, Sancta Dei Genitrix ..." "We fly to your patronage, O Holy Mother of God; despise not our petitions in our necessities, but deliver us from all dangers, O ever Glorious and Blessed Virgin" (Ancient Marian Hymn).

The idea of a patron saint still survives today in an attenuated form, but the full richness of the Roman practice can help explain the role of saints in the Church. In ancient Rome, patronage was a formal arrangement in which a powerful person would promote the welfare of a less powerful person, and in exchange the client would do whatever service the patron needed. Patronage relationships promoted solidarity between those of unequal power or status, binding together the weak and the strong and keeping Roman society unified despite socioeconomic inequality. Clients were even considered as minor members of the patron's family.

God loves Mary, though not just with the natural love of a son for his mom, or a husband for his wife, or a father for his daughter. God's love for Mary is primarily because she heard the word of God and did it, because she said yes to everything

God asked of her and identified her will with his. She made possible God's great act of mercy by cooperating in his plan and continued to cooperate no matter how much God asked of her. He gave her the dignity of being Queen of Heaven and is willing to grant her any request she makes.

As such a powerful patron, Mary is able to respond to any privation or deficiency that her clients and spiritual children suffer. And as a member of the human race, she has the solidarity with us to be merciful.

Mary's power is dependent on Jesus' covenant and the graces that his sacrifice earned from the Father. But the tradition of the Church emphasizes that Mary is also merciful in her own name, and not just in Jesus' name. She is "Comforter of the Afflicted" and "Help of Christians" and "Our Lady of Perpetual Help." It is her own "eyes of mercy" that turn toward us poor, banished children of Eve in our exile. Her power is not her own, but Jesus delegates to her the power to distribute the graces he earned through his sacrifice. There is a long history of God delegating spiritual power to particular helpers:

- Moses delegates his spiritual power to seventy-two judges (Num 11:24–30);
- Elijah gives a double portion of his spirit to his successor the prophet Elisha (2 Kings 2:9);
- Jesus delegates spiritual power to his apostles (Lk 9:1–6) and his seventy-two disciples (Lk 10:1–12); and
- Jesus delegates the power to determine what God will count as a sin in Heaven—first to Saint Peter (Mt 16:19) and then after the Resurrection, to the Church (Jn 20:23).

In the same way, the Church teaches that Jesus delegates to Mary the power to help, to show mercy to anyone in need who asks for it.

The Heavenly Lady Appearing on Earth

Mary responds to our larger needs as well as our smaller needs, perhaps most spectacularly through her apparitions. Earlier we discussed the argument of Joseph Cardinal Ratzinger (before he became Pope Benedict XVI) that categorized visions such as Fatima, Lourdes, and Guadalupe as instances of prophecy that respond to the necessities of the times. These interventions qualify as merciful acts—and on a grand scale at that—since they responded to the deficiencies and needs of the Church in a particular time and place.

In Mexico, the Church was largely unsuccessful in her attempts to bring the Gospel to the Aztecs and other indigenous peoples, with cultural misunderstandings on both sides creating enormous obstacles to trust. The apparitions at Guadalupe overcame all that misunderstanding. Our Lady appeared to an Aztec Christian, spoke in his language, and left on Saint Juan Diego's tilma the image of Mary as an indigenous woman. After that, the number of converts to the Church in the New World went from a handful of people to the millions.

The French Revolution was an atheistic and violently anti-Catholic regime that suppressed the Church and killed priests and religious during its Reign of Terror. Even after it ended, disdain for Catholic piety and hatred of the Church remained widespread. In response, our Lady appeared to visionaries in France several times during the nineteenth century: to Saint Catherine Labouré in 1830, which promoted the Miraculous Medal and devotion to the Heart of Mary; in La Salette to two children, Maximin Giraud and Mélanie Calvat, in 1846; to Saint Bernadette Soubirous at Lourdes in 1858; and at Pontmain to two boys, Joseph and Eugene Barbadette, and to other children as well, in 1871. These apparitions contradicted the secular mindset of the Church's enemies and strengthened the faith of the French people.

In 1917, the Bolshevik Communists overthrew the Russian government and unleashed another virulently atheistic state, the Soviet Union. In response, on the other side of Europe, our Lady appeared in Fatima, Portugal, to Saints Jacinta and Francisco Marto and their cousin Lucia Santos, and she encouraged them to pray for the conversion of Russia and ask the pope to consecrate Russia to Mary's Immaculate Heart. In 1984, Pope Saint John Paul II consecrated the world to Mary, which Sister Lucia, the last surviving member of the three visionaries, said later had fulfilled the conditions our Lady had set.[1] In 1987–1988, Pope Saint John Paul II called for a Marian year: less than three months after it had finished, the Berlin Wall fell.

The bigger the problem we see in the world, the more supernatural a solution is needed. Mary's extraordinary love earns her the ability to exercise extraordinary grace.

The Mother of Mercy

According to the Second Vatican Council's Dogmatic Constitution on the Church, *Lumen Gentium* (November 21, 1964),

> Mary, a daughter of Adam, consenting to the divine Word, became the mother of Jesus, the one and only Mediator. Embracing God's salvific will with a full heart and impeded

---

1   "On 25 March 1984 in Saint Peter's Square, while recalling the *fiat* uttered by Mary at the Annunciation, the Holy Father, in spiritual union with the Bishops of the world, who had been 'convoked' beforehand, entrusted all men and women and all peoples to the Immaculate Heart of Mary. ... Sister Lucia personally confirmed that this solemn and universal act of consecration corresponded to what Our Lady wished (*'Sim, està feita, tal como Nossa Senhora a pediu, desde o dia 25 de Março de 1984'*: 'Yes it has been done just as Our Lady asked, on 25 March 1984': Letter of 8 November 1989)." Congregation for the Doctrine of the Faith, introduction to *The Message of Fatima*, by Archbishop Tarcisio Bertone; http://www.vatican.va/roman_curia/congregations /cfaith/documents/rc_con_cfaith_doc_20000626_message-fatima_en.html.

by no sin, she devoted herself totally as a handmaid of the Lord to the person and work of her Son, under Him and with Him, by the grace of almighty God, serving the mystery of redemption. Rightly therefore the holy Fathers see her as used by God not merely in a passive way, but as freely cooperating in the work of human salvation through faith and obedience. (56)

"Salve Regina, Mater Misericordiae"—"Hail, Holy Queen, Mother of Mercy." Many of the titles of Mary fittingly reflect her relationship to her Son. She is the "Mirror of Justice" because her Son is justice incarnate; since she is the source of his body, he takes after her in his human features, and so her face and his share the same image. Similarly, since he is mercy incarnate, and she is his mother, she is Mother of Mercy.

But her bearing Jesus in the flesh, being the source of the *carnis* in the Incarnation, only scratches the surface of Mary's importance. Jesus hints at this when he corrects the woman who praises his mother merely for her contribution to his human nature: " 'Blessed is the womb that carried you and the breasts at which you nursed.' He replied, 'Rather, blessed are those who hear the word of God and observe it' " (Lk 11:27–28). Earlier in Luke's Gospel, Jesus had made the point that his family is made up of those who keep God's commandments: "My mother and my brothers are those who hear the word of God and act on it" (Lk 8:21). Mary is not the Mother of Mercy solely because she carried Jesus in her womb. She is also Jesus' mother because she listens for the word of God, consents to it perfectly, and acts on it. The Second Vatican Council sees Mary not as a passive bystander to Jesus' life, but "as freely cooperating in the work of human salvation through faith and obedience" (*Lumen Gentium*, no. 56).

Mary's response to Saint Gabriel, "Let it be done to me," her *fiat*, is not merely giving God the green light to do with her as he wills. She is actively assenting to God's action, trusting in him, aligning her will with his. Mary's being full of grace means that she is able to love God the way all of us ought to love God, simply because he is all good and deserving of all our love, without concern for what he does or does not do to us. Mary does not make deals with God; she never negotiates ("I'll bear your child, but what is in it for me?"). She trusts him, and so follows him: "Thy will be done on earth as it is in Heaven."

Mary still had one great act of surrender to make to God, at the foot of the Cross. It is clear that Jesus' suffering comes at God's command. In fact, Jesus echoes his mother's *fiat* both in his agony in Gethsemane ("not my will but yours be done" [Lk 22:42]) and again from the Cross ("Father, into your hands I commend my spirit" [Lk 23:46]). At the foot of the Cross, Mary has to pronounce another *fiat*, this time not to a miraculous baby boy but to his torture and death at God's command. Mary suffers at Jesus' suffering most profoundly, but nonetheless she renews her Yes to God—"yes, this sacrifice is necessary; yes, because it is your will. I am not angry at this suffering, even though it pierces my heart. Thy will be done, and may my will be joined to yours."

Earlier we pointed out that holiness is defined as having our wills identified with God's so that we love what he loves because he loves it. Mary's Yes at Calvary was in some sense her supreme act of holiness, her most difficult act of trust in God and consent to his will. Jesus said that the one who hears the word of God and does it is his mother; in some sense, when Mary consents to the Crucifixion, she is at that moment the Mother of God the most. And since she is consenting to the sacrifice that seals the New Covenant, the great act of mercy and reconciliation with God, when she consents to her Son's sacrifice, she is at that moment most the Mother of Mercy.

"Mary's Faith Gave Human Flesh to Jesus"

According to Pope Francis, in his Address on Marian Prayer, October 12, 2013, "Mary's faith gave human flesh to Jesus." He continues,

> What took place most singularly in the Virgin Mary also takes place within us, spiritually, when we receive the word of God with a good and sincere heart and put it into practice. It is as if God takes flesh within us; he comes to dwell in us, for he dwells in all who love him and keep his word.... It means giving him our hands, to caress the little ones and the poor; our feet, to go forth and meet our brothers and sisters; our arms, to hold up the weak and to work in the Lord's vineyard, our minds, to think and act in the light of the Gospel; and especially to offer our hearts to love and to make choices in accordance with God's will. All this happens thanks to the working of the Holy Spirit. And in this way we become instruments in God's hands, so that Jesus can act in the world through us.

Mary is the Mother of the Church and the Mother of Mercy. She is the first person to say yes to Jesus. She is the New Eve: where Eve means "mother of all the living" (Gen 3:20), Mary is the mother of all those brought back to spiritual life, the mother of all those conceived by the Holy Spirit (who is "the Giver of Life" as we say in the Creed). She is our mother, and we are her children. We should strive to be like her in her virtues, including in her mercy.

Mercy requires that we have solidarity with others, that we notice their needs, and that we are able and willing to help. Mary's awareness of the needs of others is clear from the wedding feast at Cana; we too should notice the privations of others and seek to help them. Mary's power, as we have said, comes from her close unity with her Son; no matter how much skill or knowledge or wealth we have in a worldly sense, there is no greater source of powerful goodness than Christ.

After giving them his spiritual power, Jesus tells the disciples, "Whoever listens to you listens to me" (Lk 10:16). In an even greater way, Mary's complete unity with her Son means that whoever imitates her imitates Christ as well. We can imitate Mary in her faith, her Yes to God in all things, even in her suffering. And by echoing her Yes, we too can be united to our Lord's sacrifice on the Cross, be brought into his covenant, and have our hearts renewed by his mercy.

Acknowledgments

This book is the product of over twenty years of thinking about justice and mercy and God's attributes—which means there are a lot of people to thank.

First, I would like to thank my students at MIT, who attended several "Tech Catholic Talks" on themes that I worked into this book. Their questions and feedback helped me realize weaknesses in my presentation. Their prayers and support for my ministry have been priceless.

In August of 2015, the monks of the Monastery of Christ in the Desert invited me to give a week's worth of lectures on mercy and its relationship to the Rule of Saint Benedict. That was when I first organized many of my academic ideas about mercy into a more pastoral form—and got the idea for Brother Tardy. I would like to thank Abbot Philip Lawrence, O.S.B., for the opportunity.

In May 2015, Father Stephane Baek hosted me at the Catholic University of Seoul to give lectures on Saint Anselm and mercy, which pushed me to sharpen many points that appear in this book.

This book is part of a series entitled "What Every Catholic Should Know", but several non-Catholics have played major parts in the ideas found here. When I was an undergraduate at Yale, Marilyn McCord Adams taught me Saint Anselm's work, for which I'm eternally grateful; and Nicholas Woltersorff taught me about the problem of divine names in the classical concept of God, which has shaped my thinking deeply ever since. These themes take prominence in chapter 1, but are present throughout. At the Heritage Foundation, I was honored to work with Robert Rector, the universally acknowledged architect of the Personal Responsibility and Work Opportunity Reconciliation Act (the famous 1996 welfare reform law), which showed that well-designed public policy could achieve the goals of mercy. While he wasn't the inspiration of the merciful curmudgeon I use as an example in chapter 1, that certainly describes him.

First Things and the Institute on Religion and Public Life taught me how to be a writer and a public intellectual—and an adult. Many parts of this book got their start from my experiences there from 1998 to 2001. For example, although Reinhold Niebuhr was a major influence on *First Things* from its inception, Matt Berke got me especially interested in Niebuhr with his long conversations about his favorite author. Because of the Institute's Ramsey colloquia, I got to meet (experience?) Stanley Hauerwas, which led me both to be fascinated by his pacifism and provoked (if not always convinced) by his antipathy to Niebuhr's position. Also, Father Richard John Neuhaus sent me on assignment to cover a conference on faith-based charities, which got me interested in the work of John DiIulio and related thinkers who saw welfare policy and criminal justice reform as hard-nosed examples of mercy in public policy.

Once I left *First Things* to return to graduate school, Father Neuhaus encouraged me to continue contributing, which allowed me to publish an earlier version of some of the themes of this book ("The Tribunal of Mercy", March 2003). Relatedly, Matt Boudway's invitation when he was an editor at *Crisis* to review Hauerwas' Gifford Lectures helped me think through the issues I deal with in chapter 2. In the post-Neuhaus era of *First Things*, Rusty Reno and Matt Schmitz helped sharpen a would-be review essay of Walter Cardinal Kasper's book on mercy into a much more powerful (and shorter) review ("What Mercy Is", March 2015)—which became the basis of chapter 1. More fundamentally, Father Neuhaus served as an inspiration (and later midwife) for my priestly vocation, first showing me how a diocesan priest could also be an intellectual, and then helping me enter seminary.

His Eminence Sean P. O'Malley, O.F.M., accepted me into the seminary, even though I had never lived in Boston; ordained me to the priesthood in 2010; appointed me to the university chaplaincy work that I love; and has throughout been the model of a prayerful and merciful shepherd.

Bishop Mark O'Connell, auxiliary bishop for the Archdiocese of Boston, was a newly minted canon lawyer in 2002, when the abuse crisis in Boston broke, and was part of the team of archdiocesan canon lawyers working on the canonical side to deal with accused priests. He's been one of the most informed observers of the crisis for years, having had to examine or oversee hundreds of case files. In a conversation, I shared with him my thoughts about how a misunderstanding of mercy contributed to the abuse crisis—and then he found them so helpful that he started "market testing" them as he spoke to audiences around the country. I might not have included chapter 7 without his encouragement.

David O'Connor directed my dissertation, providing me with gentle guidance that allowed me to be creative and ambitious with my ideas. Somehow, a project that began with "let's test out Saint Anselm's theory of divine language regarding justice" grew into a wide-ranging, but surprisingly powerful, reflection on contemporary liberal theory and the weakness of tolerance as a concept, as well as a reflection on criminal justice, punishment, and the philosophy of law. His own work on the differences between Plato's and Aristotle's theories of justice helped me to realize that Platonic theories of justice might be more congenial to theories of mercy than I had realized.

When you hang around universities long enough, your teachers can become your friends—and your friends, teachers. Gyula Klima taught me medieval philosophy at Yale and Notre Dame, and he continues to teach me whenever he writes anything. Father Romanus Cessario's work on the concept of mercy in Saint Thomas Aquinas and Cajetan was influential in writing chapter 1; his friendship and mentorship has been even more influential. Ralph McInerny was a generous teacher who encouraged my writing career and helped get me the position at *First Things*. My undergraduate friends Josh Hochschild and Eric Enlow, and my graduate friend David Thunder, are now professors in their own right and have taught me much by their own intellectual projects. Josh, Chris Blum, and Chris Mirus invited me in 2013, out of the blue, to chair a session at the American Catholic Philosophical Association (ACPA), which reintroduced me to the academic world (after my ordination had immersed me in pastoral work), giving me the confidence to start reading and writing academically again. Monte Brown has encouraged me to write and speak on Anselm and mercy, even organizing an ACPA session and devoting an issue of the *St. Anselm Journal* to that theme.

Robert P. George's James Madison Program at Princeton and Luis Tellez and the Witherspoon Institute co-hosted my postdoc year at Princeton, which gave me the opportunity to meet many top political thinkers and deepen my intellectual engagement with liberalism. In particular, I would like to thank Stephen Macedo at Princeton's Center for Human Values, who, while he might not have been excited at my views, nonetheless consistently and fair-handedly included me in the stimulating conversations and dinners that his center hosted.

It was on the way to the airport after the ACPA that Chris Blum mentioned the possibility of writing this book. Without him and his team at the Augustine Institute, I would never have sat down to write this. The Fellowship of Catholic

University Students invited me to their summer staff training for three weeks in 2018 to serve as a chaplain, which gave me the perfect setup to write the early drafts of many chapters here. Thanks also to Father Fessio and Mark Brumley at Ignatius Press, to series editor Joseph Pearce, and to all my editors who always made things better.

A lot of acknowledgments by an author talk about how writing requires patience from the friends and family of the author; I didn't really understand that until now. My brother priests at the rectory put up with my disappearing for hours to write; with my frazzled appearance when I emerged to grab something to eat; and with my less than fully present conversations when our mealtimes synchronized. Father Darin Colarusso and Father Greg Vozzo were functionally "unfriended" during that time—and still made efforts to reach out to me. They don't realize how much they helped. I had to skip my usual summertime visits to my family outside of Boston, which I hated but was necessary. I am grateful to them in so many ways.

I especially would like to thank our Lady, the Mirror of Justice and Mother of Mercy, who has prayed for this sinner every time I needed her to.